STATEMENT

THE BEN MOON STORY

Ed Douglas

STATEMENT
THE BEN MOON STORY

Published by Vertebrate Publishing, Sheffield.
www.v-publishing.co.uk

STATEMENT
THE BEN MOON STORY

First published in 2015 by Vertebrate Publishing.

Vertebrate Publishing
Crescent House, 228 Psalter Lane, Sheffield S11 8UT.
www.v-publishing.co.uk

Cover photo: Ray Wood.

A CIP catalogue record for this book is available from the British Library.

ISBN: 978-1-906148-98-0 (Hardback)
ISBN: 978-1-906148-99-7 (Ebook)

Design and production by Nathan Ryder.
Vertebrate Graphics Limited.
www.v-graphics.co.uk

Vertebrate Publishing is committed to printing on paper from sustainable sources.

MIX
Paper from
responsible sources
FSC
www.fsc.org   FSC® C013056

Printed and bound in the UK by T. J. International Ltd, Padstow, Cornwall.

CONTENTS

AUTHOR'S NOTE

This is the latest book in a recent series about the leading climbers of the 1980s and 1990s and the third published by Vertebrate, following the memoirs of Jerry Moffatt and Ron Fawcett. My original plan was to write these memoirs as a first-person autobiography, in a similar way to those of Moffatt and Fawcett, but it quickly became obvious to me that this wouldn't work for Ben Moon. Ben's father Jeremy was an important part of his story and yet Ben barely knew him from first-hand experience and it seemed unnatural to tell Jeremy's story in this way. Then there was the complication of Ben's own writings, his letters and occasional articles, which are thoughtful, inquiring and often stylish – and in direct contrast to his approach to interviews which is direct and laconic. Matching these together struck me as too artificial, and showed me that had he the time and inclination, Ben would be perfectly capable of writing his own story in his own voice. So this book is an authorised biography, giving Ben's version of events only, especially of matters related to climbing. Occasionally, when his memory proved especially vague, I sought help from others, but only in relation to more personal matters.

Ed Douglas
Sheffield, December 2014

Climbers on the Inaccessible Pinnacle, Sgùrr Dearg, Isle of Skye, in the 1930s.
Photo: Jack Moon/Moon Family Collection.

PROLOGUE

In early 1944, the Scottish climber W. H. Murray, then incarcerated in a German prisoner-of-war camp near the Czechoslovakian town of Mährisch Trübau, began work for the second time on his book *Mountaineering in Scotland*. His first manuscript, written on toilet paper donated by the Red Cross, had just been confiscated by the Gestapo. Half starved, but with access to paper and a library in which to work, Murray was actually relieved to be starting again. This time, he promised himself, he would write a book that was less about extreme climbs and insouciance in the face of danger, and more about the 'feeling for beauty' mountains inspire. He opened his book in the Cuillin mountains of Skye, which he had explored thoroughly in the 1930s, a place and time of complete freedom recalled from prison and the depths of war. If you wanted to find the soul of British climbing, you could do worse than to start looking among the Cuillins.

The camp, covered in snow, was set in woodland and the light was often flat and grey, which might explain Murray's intense description of dawn over the mountains: 'The grey sky was steadily changing to cornflower blue and black rock to ashen. To obtain a still finer vantage point we moved east to Sgurr a'Mhadaidh. No sooner did we reach the top than the sun rose. Down in the basin of Coruisk, the cloud-surface at once flashed into flame, as though a stupendous crucible were filled with burning silver. The twenty turrets of the Cuillin, like islands lapped by fire-foam, flushed faintly pink. The shade crimsoned. Within a space of minutes, the rocks had run the gamut of autumn leafage, "yellow, and black, and pale, and hectic red." Beyond such bare words one may say little. The mind fails one, miserably and painfully, before great beauty. It cannot understand. Yet it would contain more.'

More than sixty years after Murray wrote these words, a small gang of friends set out in similar spirit from Glen Brittle in the pre-dawn light to walk the length of the Cuillin ridge. Their plan, if you can call it a plan, since that requires actual planning, would take them up into Coir' a' Ghrunnda and the summit of Sgurr Dubh an Da Bheinn on the ridge proper. From there they would walk to the ridge's most easterly summit, Gars-Bheinn, work their way back and, after taking in the summit of Sgurr Dubh Mor, continue along the ridge, scrambling across Murray's 'twenty turrets', towards the finish at Sgurr nan Gillean.

First they had to overcome the famous Thearlaich-Dubh gap, a notch in the ridge you abseil into and climb out of at the moderate standard of Very Difficult, although it is wickedly polished now, unlike in Murray's day. Still, there can have been few parties in the history of mountaineering so qualified to overcome this particular challenge, even if, in all honesty, they weren't sufficiently fit for the rest of it. Chris Plant, Derbyshire born, quiet and well liked, someone who had started climbing in the traditional way, had worked his way through the grades and in the late 1980s was suddenly one of the best rock climbers in the country. Except that Plant Pot, as he is universally known, stumbled on the path up to Coir' a' Ghrunnda and injured himself. You go on, he said to the rest of the party, without me. No matter: there was still no shortage of talent. Ben Tetler remains an almost mythical figure in British rock climbing – not least for his astonishing solo ascent in 1999 of the Curbar frightener *Knockin' on Heaven's Door* – with a deep interest in political economy, prompting him to call a new route at the Staffordshire Roaches *The Spectatorship of the Proletariat*. Ben Pritchard had climbed all kinds of challenges, from the hardest boulder problems to the big walls of Yosemite, often in his professional role of climbing cameraman and filmmaker, one of the best and best known in Britain.

Then there was the star of the group and the subject of this book – Ben Moon, just past his forty-first birthday. Had you been reading climbing magazines in the mid 1980s, you would not have predicted his presence on the Cuillin ridge twenty years later. His style was about as far removed from the purple dreamy prose of Murray as it was possible to get; a punk-rock fan with a wild hairdo and a terse way of speaking his mind. He was for some the epitome of the sport-climbing revolution then engulfing British climbing, a process that would, according to some, undermine the very foundations of everything that was valuable about the sport. From this distance in time, it is hard to believe the level of hostility aimed at sport climbing. He and his cohort were routinely described as soulless. By focusing on the difficulty of a climb, by making it safe so a sequence of moves could be practised again and again, Ben Moon was destroying something fundamentally important to earlier generations. Climbing would be, quite literally in the minds of some critics, emasculated.

Ben didn't feel the need to explain himself. Most of those criticising had little conception of what he was about. On the few occasions early in his climbing career when people got around to asking Ben what drove him, he seemed to invite hostility: 'I don't climb to be in pretty places,' he once said, which drove those nurtured on the romanticism of W. H. Murray to distraction. Had they dug a little deeper, they would have discovered the young revolutionary was as inspired by the romance and freedom of the hills as anyone else. The aesthetic of climbing, the beauty of a great line, the shapes a climber's body could make, all these were of interest to him, of far more interest than grades or sponsorship deals.

Critics argued that by using bolts to protect climbs, Ben and his kind had robbed rock climbing of its psychological interest; that their version of the sport was simply a physical challenge. If, after reading this book, you still believe that to be true, then it has failed. The threat of physical injury was largely removed, that's incontrovertible, but the psychological pressure of completing a project right at the limits of what's possible is intense, and in the 1980s it was still barely understood. Ben wasn't just one of the first redpoint climbers in history, he was and remains one of the best, in the same class as Wolfgang Güllich, the equivalent in the modern era of Chris Sharma or Adam Ondra. His realised projects, such as *Sea of Tranquility*, are still considered desperately hard almost a quarter of a century after they were first climbed.

His ascent of *Hubble* in 1990 was a step so far into the unknown that no one, not even Ben, realised how far – it is likely to have been the first 9a in history. His strength, ability and focus were so intense that sport climbing in the UK stalled for a while after Ben's generation. Surpassing what had been done was just too much to contemplate. Not only did Ben adopt and then master this new form of climbing, he did it again in the 1990s in transforming the art of bouldering into a branch of climbing that was instantly appealing, democratic and cool. As it turned out, sport climbing and bouldering didn't destroy the best traditions of British climbing. They just made British climbing bigger.

Behind his athletic brilliance, behind the guesswork and hostility around how he climbed, Ben Moon's story is far richer and more complex than those who rejected the sport-climbing project could possible have imagined. He was most often compared to his near-contemporary Jerry Moffatt, but while they shared a usually friendly rivalry that pushed them to try harder, Ben's personality, background and motivation were fundamentally different. On his shelves are tomes just as venerable and inspiring as *Mountaineering in Scotland*, a gift from his grandfather who was a contemporary of Murray's and a keen amateur climber himself, who had climbed on Skye and took a great interest and pleasure in his grandson's success. On the walls of Ben's family home are some favourite works by his father, the artist Jeremy Moon. Jeremy's legacy is also

Ben in the Sheffield Polytechnic cafeteria on Broomgrove Road.
Photo: Ben Moon Collection.

important in Ben's story, as it was for his brother Rob, also on Skye that day to try the Cuillin Ridge.

They finished it, eventually, although Ben backed off leading *Naismith's Route* and they were forced to doss out for the night, still short of Am Basteir. He joked afterwards it was the hardest thing he'd ever done. Stumbling towards the Sligachan Hotel, footsore and parched, it must have felt that way. He must also have felt a connection to his grandfather, more than seventy years on from his own blissful summer days there. And had any of those who once regarded Ben as the unacceptable face of modern climbing met him coming down, it might have caused them to reconsider – like seeing Joe Strummer in St Paul's Cathedral.

Perhaps this book will change at least some of their minds about what climbing can be.

Ben in Jeremy's studio on Latchmere Road. **Photo:** Moon Family Collection.

HOOP-LA

'The real art isn't in the revolution, it's in the evolution, that's what Jeremy would say.'

David Moon is sitting in the living room of the semi-detached house his older brother Jeremy bought half a century ago to raise his family and in which to paint. Outside, the grid of suburban streets expands around the house, ending abruptly to the north and east where Kingston upon Thames meets the expanse of Richmond Park. To the west is the Thames itself and to the south, Kingston's town centre and the railway station. It's here, in suburbia, where Ben Moon was born in 1966.

The town has been commuter belt for almost as long as such a thing has existed – almost, but not quite. When the railway boom got underway, landowners in Kingston were reluctant to make room for such a noisy and dangerous experiment, not when the coaching industry was so important to the local economy. So the London and Southampton Railway was diverted a mile to the south and the first local station was called New Kingston, or Kingston-upon-Railway. When Kingston finally got its own station, New Kingston reverted to the name of the nearby hamlet of Surbiton.

London's suburbs are human life demarcated by the working day, by train timetables and bus routes, and the muted whine of jets sinking towards Heathrow. They are a place just off-stage, somewhere to change your costume and return to the spotlight, somewhere to wash your car at the weekend, where the state schools are good enough to send your kids, where the parks are large enough to qualify as a facsimile of countryside – a notion geographers term subtopia.

We like to characterise the geometric acres of near-identical houses and predictable behaviour we associate with suburbia as being toxic for creative minds. It breeds a kind of idiosyncratic resistance. On television, in its most benign form, it's the self-sufficiency of 1970s show *The Good Life*. A little more darkly, it's the secrets and sex of *Desperate Housewives*. In the late 1970s the bored resentment of punk was, quite literally, in the case of Camberley band The Members, the sound of the suburbs.

The antidote to that trope, novelist J. G. Ballard, lived until his death a few miles to the west of Kingston, down the branch line in Shepperton. Ballard spent most of his working life anatomising modernity and the dehumanising impacts of technology and a compromised environment.

Ballard used to tell newspaper interviewers who arrived from the metropolis marvelling at the somnolent world this most contemporary of novelists inhabited that he came because of the space and quiet – and to monitor the flickering pulse of the middle classes. When his wife died unexpectedly, leaving him a widower with three young children, he stayed put to raise his family and focus on his work.

He also understood that his sight of the world, which he articulated in his books, was a thin flame easily extinguished. Being in the middle of everything and competing with others can be a terrible distraction from the process of observing. The myriad versions of human experience can crowd in, muscling what you were trying to say to one side. Most of us are simply copying machines, and not even very good ones. Imagining something new, and being able to realise it, takes confidence and absolute concentration.

Focus is necessarily a constant theme in this book, albeit in the context of rock climbing and not art. Although it is perhaps less certain than many suppose where the boundaries between these two activities lie. We associate sport with hard work and practice; habits that make movement routine, hardwired in our brains, bodies that are trained to perform to their maximum potential.

The nature of creative genius is more of a mystery. It's perceived as a divine spark that changes base metal to gold. It adds glamour and excitement. Architecture seems creative in a way that engineering does not. Poets draw attention in a way copywriters don't. Yet the boundaries between what is creative and what is not are less obvious than we often assume.

For the Greeks, there was only one truly creative process, albeit not in the romantic sense we understand: *poiesis*, from which we derive the word poetry. Art and music were merely *techne*, the physical making of things by the application of rules, and consequently best left to artisans from the lower social orders.

We don't see it this way. Our culture venerates artists and musicians as much as or even more so than poets. Yet, like the Greeks, we limit ourselves with our own set of arbitrary boundaries. The idea there might be something creative in an activity like rock climbing would seem alien to many rock climbers, let alone the public. But, for the purposes of this book, and the telling of the life of Ben Moon, allow for the possibility that the states of mind in which great art is produced may be similar to that of a rock climber finally solving a sequence of moves on rock of the utmost difficulty.

Johnny Dawes is a friend and contemporary of Ben Moon, part of a generation that transformed climbing arguably more than any other. Dawes is a climber of a different mettle – fluid, mercurial, instinctive – but when asked whether climbing holds any resemblance to dance, he offered an answer touching on self-expression that could apply equally to Ben Moon or any other climber as it does to himself:

'Any time you move, your emotional state is shown in your movement. So when you move on rock it makes you remember who you are. Climbing, like dancing, reminds me of who I am and gives me hope and affection for the world. Mozart's music sounds like some form of astro-nomical maths transposed into sound. If you climb well, or if you dance well, it reconnects you with the person you really are.'

Ben's father Jeremy Moon was a young abstract artist who came to prominence in the Young Contemporaries exhibition at the RBA[1] Galleries in 1962, just a year after enrolling at the Central School of Art in Holborn. By the time he moved to Kingston in the early summer of 1966, he'd got married, to Beth, and she had given birth to their first son, Robert. Their second son, Benedick, was born two weeks after they moved in, at home in their bedroom.

Artistically, Jeremy's life was also on the upswing. During 1966 his work was shown in galleries around the world – Minneapolis, Seattle, Washington, Vancouver, Ottawa, Milan – and he was preparing a new solo show in London. He needed space for a growing family and also somewhere he could build a studio large enough to cope with the scale of his ambitious work.

Jeremy does not fit the popular image of a tortured artist. 'Jeremy was good fun,' his brother David says. 'I never think of him as being moody or depressed. Our father Jack was. Jeremy was more like our mother Ruth.'

Yet if Jeremy was more level headed and calmly focused than his father, it took him a while to find his path. This was largely to do with expectations of class and what he perceived as the wishes of his parents. He was born in the affluent Cheshire market town of Altrincham in the summer of 1934. His father, Jack, was a lawyer in Manchester – 'a good old-fashioned family solicitor' as David puts it. After Jeremy came Penny, then David, eight years younger than his brother, followed finally by Diana, twelve years Jeremy's junior. Both boys were entered for Shrewsbury School where their father had gone, and their grandfather before him.

---

1 Royal Society of British Artists.

'Father was a frustrated engineer,' David says. 'He would like to have been in manufacturing and was actually director of a small horticultural engineering company. He loved all that. Liked cars as well.' A love of cars and motorbikes is something that links all three generations: grandfather, father, uncle and son. Jack's 'pride and joy' was an Allard roadster but Jeremy arguably carried his passion further than all of them. He had a Morgan for a while in the late 1950s, and a one-cylinder Isetta, a bubble car, which he drove around Europe. And there is a blend of joy and envy on David's face when he describes the 1932 2-litre Lagonda Continental Jeremy owned: 'That was a beautiful car. It had mudguards connected to the front wheels so when you turned them, the mudguards turned too.'

Jeremy also loved motorbikes and took David on track days at Oulton Park in Cheshire and Brands Hatch. 'I remember he borrowed my one-piece suit,' David says. 'He had a heavy crash and it came back scratched. He said: "What are you complaining about? Now it looks like the genuine article."'

Parenthood curtailed Jeremy's passion for bikes, albeit temporarily. Not long before Rob was born in 1964, he went out for a final blast around London before selling his beloved Norton only for the police to pull him over for speeding. He explained the situation and the police waved him on with the suggestion that a prospective father might go more carefully. After the move to Kingston, from Swiss Cottage in north-west London where he and Beth had been living with Rob, Jeremy had bikes again to commute into central London where he was teaching at Saint Martins and then at the Chelsea School of Art.

He bought a new Honda 125 in 1972, 'a fabulous little bike', according to David, but graduated soon after to a 350cc two-stroke Kawasaki triple with the characteristic double exhaust, notorious for being the fastest bike for its engine size, and equally notorious for being difficult to handle. 'Nothing happened until you got the revs up,' David recalled, 'but after that it just took off. That was the last one.'

Jack Moon didn't just hand down his passion for speed and engines. He was a zealous golfer, playing off a handicap of just three, although, as the antithesis of the clubbable man, he couldn't stand the social life of his golf club in Hale. Jeremy also played as a boy, as would Ben when his climbing career began to wind down. In a letter to Ben, Jack recalled Jeremy playing as a junior member: 'In fact, it was at Hale Golf Course that his appendix blew up, and he had to struggle back to Glenwood and the surgeon carried him into his own car and straight to hospital and operated immediately.'

Golf wasn't Jack's only passion. He also had a great love of mountains and mountaineering, ignited by another curious link between art and climbing. 'I first got really bitten with climbing when I read Oppenheimer's *The Heart of Lakeland*,' he wrote to Ben in 1991, towards the end of his life. Lehmann Oppenheimer's 1908 account is one of the early classics of rock-climbing literature capturing the spirit of the times – fugs of pipe smoke, damp tweeds and such irascible luminaries as Oscar Eckenstein, inventor of the modern crampon, introduced by Lehman in the guise of 'The Wanderer'.

Oppenheimer's book was published towards the end of the heyday of the community of climbers that developed the sport in its earliest days. This was the era of gully climbing, of John Buckingham's hemp ropes and the strict commandment that the leader must not fall. It is hard to conceive of a climbing world of greater contrast to that epitomised by Ben Moon, and yet this was the book his grandfather gave him as Ben's early interest in climbing developed, and which he still cherishes.

Its focus was Wasdale Head and the Wastwater Hotel, and many of its principals were drawn from the professional classes of Manchester that Jack Moon knew well. There were the five Hopkinson brothers, all eminent figures, and their cousins and near-neighbours from Alderley Edge, the Pilkingtons. As climbing historian Alan Hankinson put it: 'They went to church each Sunday, read the *Manchester Guardian* and were taken to

The *Direct Route* on the Eastern Buttress, Sron na Ciche, Isle of Skye, in the 1930s.
Photo: Jack Moon/Moon Family Collection.

Hallé Orchestra concerts but never to the theatre. They epitomised the earnest, responsible, confident, thrusting spirit of the time.'

Jack Moon's climbing experiences came long after this initial phase of the sport's development, but something of the philosophy of that first wave, which was circumspect in publicising its activity and largely inclusive, is apparent in his letters to Ben: 'Our approach to climbing was quite different. We used to go in groups and climb with people of quite different standards – totally uncompetitive but wonderful, with the joy of just being there with good companions, and surrounded by a mountain landscape. Happy days indeed.'

Lehmann Oppenheimer didn't just write about this eccentric flowering of Lake District climbing, he was an active participant, particularly in Buttermere, devoting a chapter in *The Heart of Lakeland* to the protracted first ascent of Stack Ghyll on Haystacks, completed on New Year's Eve, 1900.

He was also a gifted mosaic artist and exhibitor at the Royal Academy, taking over the family business established by his father Ludwig. A beautiful example of the firm's work is in the Honan Chapel, University of Cork, a late flowering of the Irish Arts and Crafts movement. Both Lehmann and his son, the art critic Eric Newton, fought in the Great War. Lehmann died aged forty-eight after being gassed in one of the last actions of the Somme Offensive.

In 1933, Jack Moon married Ruth, who is, at the time of writing, still active at the age of 104, recently organising a sponsored walk for charity. Ruth's father had been a Methodist minister in Hale, before moving to a church in Bournemouth, where Ruth was born in 1910 and where her father died a few years later. Her mother, a determined and enterprising woman, opened a guesthouse to support her two daughters. When doctors suggested the Dorset climate might be too enervating for Ruth's delicate older sister, she opened another guesthouse in milder Broadstairs, which she later leased to move to Wimbledon, so Ruth, a talented musician, could pursue her studies in London. When she and her mother took up an invitation to visit old friends in Hale, she met another guest – Jack Moon.

Ruth was just twenty-one when they were engaged. She shared some of her husband's enthusiasms, and tried climbing, but had passions of her own, particularly for music, playing both the piano and cello. She also practised eurhythmics, a kind of kinaesthetic approach to education and personal development, essentially experiencing rhythm through movement, a way to unleash physical creativity. During her youth, eurhythmics was at the height of its popularity and would influence her son Jeremy, and ultimately, perhaps, her grandson too.

The connection Jack had to the pioneering days of climbing and the tales they inspired was thrilling for Ben. 'We had a wedding present of a weekend at Hassness in Buttermere,' Jack wrote to him, 'which was then owned by Sydney O'Hanlon, who was a friend of my father. The present included taking another couple, one of whom, the wife, was a niece of Oppenheimer's.'

Although his grandson's commitment to the sport was immeasurably more intense and professional, and in an ethical context far removed from that of the Lake District pioneers, Ben is still fascinated by its origins and his grandfather's involvement in the sport. In the late 1980s, as he approached the height of his powers, Ben and other sport climbers were routinely condemned for undermining the foundations of the sport, for not caring about the great traditions. And yet in his letters Ben would prompt his grandfather for memories of his own brief climbing career, curtailed, as was expected in that era, by the responsibilities of marriage, career and fatherhood – the risks were simply too great to justify continuing.

Neither of Jack's sons showed great interest in their father's passion for climbing, although they both enjoyed trips to the mountains. So Ben's complete absorption in the sport was an opportunity for Jack to revisit the carefree days of his young adulthood. He gave Ben his small climbing library, treasured and now valuable books like Colin Kirkus' *Let's Go Climbing!* and W. P. Haskett Smith's *Climbing in the British Isles*. It was a way of reaching down the generations. Ben would pore over these books, and was still reading the Kirkus on a bouldering trip to Fontainebleau years later; he quizzed his grandfather about annotations in the margins that noted his own activity.

'Yes, I remember *Gillercombe Buttress,*' Jack wrote, replying to one of Ben's enquiries. 'When I joined the Fell & Rock Club, I had to submit a lot of mountain visits and climbs done, and I still have a copy at the back of an old address book. It confirms that I had a few days in the Lakes in

December 1934 and probably stayed in Langdale. I don't know why I commented 'very wet boots'! But it must have been very wet on the floor of the Combe on the way up. No, I did not lead it. My leader was my old climbing friend Frank Sugden, long since dead. He was a *natural* on rock and just **flowed** over it apparently without effort. I was 27 at the time, not far off where you are now. Who was it who said: "Young men see visions and old men dream dreams."'

The *Alpine Journal's* obituary for Sugden, who died in 1967, outlined his exceptional ability as a rock climber and also his willingness to climb with those less able: 'His outstanding characteristic was his selflessness, which showed itself in the way he devoted so much of his time to helping less talented performers, who were thus able to enjoy wider climbing horizons than would otherwise have been possible for them.'

Jack at least was one of Sugden's former climbing partners who treasured his experiences into old age. He also attempted to capture the intense emotional state the mountains provoked in him. Among the works by Jeremy Moon hung on the walls of Ben's childhood home is a more than competent painting by Jack of a mountain landscape characterised by an unexpected use of colour, partly explained by the fact that Jack was colour-blind. Yet although Jeremy's passion for art began early, it wasn't Jack who inspired him.

'Art was the thing right from the beginning. Jack wasn't a bad artist, but Peter, his uncle, was really very good,' David recalled. 'He was the city architect for Nottingham and a wonderful model maker. He drove a yellow Bentley, and I remember him making a model of it for Jeremy, with a ten-shilling note in the aluminium exhaust. Jeremy was a natural. He just picked up a pen and could draw.'

'I think it is true to say,' Jeremy said in an interview, 'that I felt art was the most important thing in life. (I don't think that now – or at least I wouldn't put it like that now.) I was musical – played the flute, but didn't get on with musicians either at school, at home or later at

Cambridge where a passionate interest in modern jazz put other forms of music out of my mind for four or five years. I think modern poetry was my first adult art experience. This was at public school. I still read a lot of poetry.'

Jeremy also played the saxophone, and his deep love and knowledge of jazz was fed by evenings at Ronnie Scott's and other jazz clubs when he worked in advertising in London. His passion for jazz is captured in a painting he did as a late teenager while at Shrewsbury of a jazz club in the style of Picasso. As pastiche goes, it is remarkably accomplished, a cubist six-piece band crammed together on a small stage in front of a packed audience, led by a clarinettist in a bright blue suit. Given Jeremy's age, the self-assurance and ability exhibited in the painting is astonishing.

He went to Cambridge from Shrewsbury, scraping in on the strength of just one A-Level – Jack was remembered with affection and gratitude at Christ's College for his footballing prowess – to read law.

'At Cambridge I knew I wanted to be an artist – not a painter, although on the strength of about six highly eclectic pictures done during those years, I was thought of as a 'painter' rather than a 'writer', a footballer etc. But I knew nothing about painting, about the history of art since Cézanne. My main beliefs at this time of my life were a simple belief in what I called existentialism and by which I meant a belief that the individual must be self-sufficient and self-actuated, and an inarticulate desire to be an artist in the future.'

He became interested in cinema and thought of becoming a filmmaker, although, as he explained, 'I didn't have any reason for making a film except the fascination of images changing within the four sides of the viewfinder – that's not film making.' But his contact in the film industry let him down, and instead he started in the advertising business, first in Manchester and then in London, at Napper, Stinton & Woolley. 'I think at this time – I was twenty-four – I was very immature emotionally and intellectually. I had hardly started. Yet contemporaries of mine at Cambridge were already writing books, editing magazines and acting in West End plays.'

Jeremy didn't, as you might assume for a talented artist, go into the creative side of advertising. He was an account man, overseeing the business and keeping clients happy. 'The thing about Jeremy,' David said, 'and here you can see some similarity with Ben, was that he was very business-like. The advertising professional knew he needed to talk to the right people. He needed to promote; he needed to push. [The] *Studio* magazine liked to interview him because he was very articulate.'

It would take Ben, who started climbing much younger than his father did his career as an artist, longer to appreciate the value of a good press. But he shared his father's instinct to bury himself at the centre of the world he wished to occupy. 'Jeremy got to know important artists like John Hoyland and kept pressure on the gallery. The paintings were bloody good but he understood that you can't wait for people to come along to buy them.'

In August 1960, Jeremy saw the pivotal abstract exhibition at the RBA Galleries called *Situation*, which galvanised new interest in abstract art and brought the names of its stars – John Hoyland, Bridget Riley and William Turnbull – to public attention. *Situation* was a step away from the abstract tradition of St Ives and a step towards the large and ambitious works then being made in America.

The wit and energy of the art on show was immensely exciting. The exhibition's catalogue quoted art critic Harold Rosenberg: 'What was to go on the canvas was not a picture but an event.' This idea in particular would resonate with Jeremy, unlocking something in his head. Now twenty-six, with school, national service in Korea, Cambridge and a couple of years in advertising behind him, he finally understood how to proceed: '[It was] like getting the whole message of what modern painting was about,' he said.

In terms of damaging your prospects, changing career midstream now isn't the risky venture it once was. Jeremy was anxious that having found a niche in the world, his parents might be alarmed at his decision to turn his back on advertising and try to make his way as an artist. (It was typical of him to embark wholeheartedly on this new venture, to shed his previous life completely rather than experiment at the weekends.) So he wrote Ruth and Jack a letter explaining his decision, which started with the words: 'Will you please sit down before you read this.'

As Jack's letters to his grandson Ben suggest, Jeremy need not have worried so much about what his father might think of his decision. 'Father would have taken a little vicarious pleasure in it,' David says. 'He would rather have liked to do something similar. Ruth would have been a bit more concerned. But in those days, if things didn't work out, you could always get another job.'

The world of work had been less forgiving in Jack's day. In the late 1980s, he would write to Ben, then embarking on the unconventional path of a professional rock climber, of the career choices he faced. 'I grew up in the days when it was customary to follow in father's footsteps, as I did, but with hindsight I realise it was his choice and not mine. But in the 1920s and 1930s there were three million unemployed and a safe haven was greatly to be desired.'

In 1961, Jeremy enrolled at the Central School of Art, embarking on a period of intense creative exploration. To begin with, he experimented in sculpture and made several works, one of which won the Associated Electrical Industries Prize for Sculpture in 1962. He also moved on swiftly from attending classes to giving them, although not at Central but at Saint Martins, quickly realising that he was much closer to realising his vision than he had anticipated.

Soon he had put sculpture to one side, although he was teaching it, and concentrated exclusively on painting. His elder son Rob, himself an artist, says that Jeremy 'hit the ground running. He was making mature works almost straight away. I think people were wondering where this person had come from.'

Jeremy in his Swiss Cottage studio, 1964. **Photo**: Tony Evans/Timelapse Library Ltd.

What characterises these early works is their bright optimism and sense of fun. 'It was terribly uplifting as you walked into his studio,' David says. 'His titles were always fun. The later paintings were cooler, more thoughtful. One of the things he loved was playing with your eyes. Your eye can't rest. It's very energetic work.'

A good example from this first period is the 1965 painting *Hoop-La*. This large, square image is a bright red field with five blue circular shapes, all but one of which appear cropped by the edge of the canvas, as though they have been thrown in the air with too much exuberance. In January 2013, *The Observer's* art critic Laura Cumming chose this work as one of ten paintings to lift the winter gloom. It's worth quoting her assessment in full:

'A burst of sudden glory – Thomas Hobbes's quirky definition of laughter – could double as a subtitle for this merry painting by the English artist Jeremy Moon. Everything is up in the air (so to speak, for this is ostensibly an abstract work) as the blue discs arc across the brilliant red canvas. Of course they seem to suggest juggler's balls, one flying out of sight but none dropping because the painting keeps them suspended forever. But this sight gag depends upon pure geometry and colour, blue leaping out of red, circle scintillating against square. In theory this is a work of hard-core abstraction; in practice it is instant uplift.'

Looking at *Hoop-La*, which is now in the Tate's collection, it's impossible not to appreciate the appeal of abstract art, and the insights it offers, even if you don't ultimately care for it. It requires a long and patient reflection on our perception of the world – of colour, shape and movement – to produce work like this, and a calm emotional maturity to keep it light and amusing. It's Zen with a sense of humour.

This aspect of movement in Jeremy Moon's work, the quality that gives it such energy, is worth examining, because it impinges in a significant way on his son's accomplishments as a rock climber. In 1961, while still working in advertising, Jeremy began taking evening classes in ballet and excelled at it. It was ludicrous to imagine that someone who took it up in his mid-twenties could expect to do it professionally, but he did contemplate trying choreography and was an admirer of George Balanchine, the Russia-born choreographer known as the father of American ballet.

The synergies between dance and climbing have already been drawn, and it's easy to overstate them. But it's also rather poignant to think of the father and a son who barely had the chance to know him both making shapes with their bodies, finding combinations of moves that are pleasing and stretching their minds through the training of their bodies. Ultimately, Jeremy's connection to dance was intense but short-lived. He was painting with confidence and producing works of maturity and Jeremy wasn't the kind of person to flit from one subject to another, putting down his flute because he couldn't devote sufficient time to it.

In 1962, some of his work was included in the Young Contemporaries exhibition at the RBA Galleries, alongside near contemporaries like David Hockney and Patrick Caulfield, and attracted attention from a new private gallery that skilfully caught the geometric wave of interest in abstract art.

The Rowan Gallery was located in the heart of Belgravia, on Lowndes Street – perhaps not the most obvious place to look for the avant-garde – and was the bold project of a former Guards officer with a well-informed passion for contemporary art. Alex Gregory-Hood was in his mid-forties, the product of minor aristocracy, with a Viceroy of India and Manchester cotton merchants in the family. He saw Jeremy's work and wrote to him, offering to sell his work.

Gregory-Hood's new venture represented a constellation of young English painters and sculptors, like the Sheffield artist Brian Fielding and the sculptor Phillip King, a student of Anthony Caro and a contemporary of Jeremy's at Christ's, where he read modern languages. King's career had been much more direct than Jeremy's; after Cambridge he had gone straight to Saint Martins and was then an assistant to Henry Moore. Moon would also become a friend of Caro's, yet another graduate of Christ's, whose understanding and enthusiasm would sustain Jeremy.

David can remember helping Jeremy hang one of his first solo shows at the Rowan Gallery and the plummy voiced Gregory-Hood sending out for fish and chips to sustain them. His brother must have been a rather dazzling figure; the sports cars and jazz clubs of the advertising years seamlessly replaced by the successful artist. And soon he was engaged as well, and contemplating family life.

Elizabeth – Beth – Bryant was a young teacher at the Mary Datchelor School in Camberwell, beginning her first proper job after a brief stint teaching English as a second language in Finland. She had grown up in Bristol, she and her identical twin Jenny the youngest of five children. Beth's father, Arthur Bryant, was a rope-maker, running a family business stretching back several generations to the early eighteenth century with a shop on Old Market Street. As the use of ropes in merchant shipping decreased, the business, run after Arthur's retirement by Beth's brothers John and Joe, diversified into caravans and awnings, and was in the 1970s scooped up by Blacks.

Beth went to St Brandon's School, was evacuated to the Bishop's House in Wells during the war and graduated from Bristol University, before moving to London, along with her twin sister, to start her career. She joined the Hampstead Choral Society, then in a period of resurgence under the baton of Martindale Sidwell, where she met Jeremy's sister Penny, who was also a member. They got on, moved into a flat together and so it was that when Jeremy knocked on his sister's door one day it was answered by the woman he would marry.

If family lore holds true, Jeremy actually took Beth's twin Jenny out on a date first, but his connection to Beth soon deepened. She was living in Belsize Park Gardens and would catch the bus to work in Camberwell, which took her down Chepstow Road in Westbourne Park, where Jeremy was then living and painting in a one-bedroom flat that he used as a studio. (He'd found the flat after coming off his motorbike outside the shop downstairs. The owner had helped him, and they got talking.)

'Sometimes,' she says with a gentle, teasing smile, 'I'd hop off the bus.' Their wedding photo shows Jeremy smiling confidently with equal measures of bohemian cool and optimism for the future.

After they married in 1963, Beth and Jeremy lived for a short while at Chepstow Road before moving to a high-ceilinged flat on King Henry's Road, a little to the south of where she had been living, and not far from Swiss Cottage. Jeremy painted huge geometric shapes on the curtains of the tall windows. Beth left her job to become a full-time mother when Rob was born in 1964.

Beth and Jeremy seemed to complement each other effortlessly. He was more ebullient, but if she was quieter, she also had a kind of stillness that spoke of immense emotional resilience. Many of the Moon clan are (or at least were, pre-computer) generous letter writers, offering each other support, advice and news. Beth was no exception. Her letters to Ben are marked by her engagement with the world, what she's reading or the music she's currently enjoying, the places or people she plans to visit. She sends him tapes of Mozart or enthuses about a trip to India. ('You can't go there and be the same person ever again. You must go there! The best thing is the people – taxi drivers, rickshaw drivers, porters, waiters, hotel managers, hotel managers' brothers, Sikhs, Hindu pilgrims, cooks, cooks' assistants, sirdars … you can't help getting involved with them all. I made a lot of friends!')

Jeremy and Ben.
Photo: Moon Family Collection.

It's invidious to judge whether Ben is more like his father or his mother but in appearance, he has a stronger resemblance to Jeremy. There is a brilliant portrait of Jeremy in his studio, taken by the Polish-born Jorge Lewinski, the pre-eminent photographer of artists from the 1960s onwards who liked to capture his famous subjects where they worked. This image of Jeremy, taken at Kingston in 1970, catches him in front of one of his paintings from that year, a series of floating grids and blocks of colour, cigarette in right hand, his left tucked into the pocket of paint-spattered trousers. His hair is long enough to be bordering on fashionable for that era, the smile still assured, despite the lines around his eyes that hadn't been there a few years before when Lewinski photographed him the first time.

That smile, however, is not Ben's. He has the quieter, softer smile of his mother. He also has the emotional resilience his mother drew on in the months and years after his father's death. Perhaps all that can be said on the subject was best expressed in a letter Ben's aunt, Jeremy's sister Penny, wrote to her nephew after a family event had brought them together in 1991. 'I was closer to [Jeremy] than anyone else I think. I have so many memories and sometimes dream about him too – seeing you yesterday brought me close to him. You are extraordinarily like him *and* Beth.'

In 1965 Jeremy created some of his most exuberant work, including *Hoop-La*, and *Eiger*, another series of blue discs escaping a square canvas that is gunmetal grey and rather forbidding. In *From Nepal*, two triangles, one of silver, the other burnt umber, are joined together so that the peak of the silver triangle points to the sky while the brown one forms a deep-cut valley. But the move to Kingston and Ben's arrival prompted a hiatus in Jeremy's work while a new studio was built in the back garden. John Hoyland had already moved nearby, and done something similar; Bernard Cohen and John Edwards would follow them.

The most important factor in choosing a house in Kingston was how big a studio you could build in the garden. Jeremy's is light and functional, although difficult and expensive to heat. But the room is still recognisably

Jeremy's, piled with canvases, his sketchbooks, in which he planned his large canvases in fine detail, often abandoning work he felt wasn't worth painting, arranged on shelves along one wall.

His work after the move to Kingston became much more geometric and ordered, his use of colour more subdued and reflective. But it was, as he had explained to his brother David, evolution, not revolution. In a letter he wrote to his sister-in-law Jenny in 1972, he wrote: 'My temperamental need for order and discipline and visual clarity always clashes with my desire to work spontaneously and more sensuously but it is necessary to know oneself in art and I think my best work so far has come out of just this contradiction. Now I am doing a series of slightly shaped very big, very simple pictures which are going well.'

Jeremy was, by his own judgement, in 'high spirits' in this dazzling letter to Jenny. 'The important thing is to keep working the way one believes in and to the best of one's ability and honestly. I must learn not to worry too much about short-term responses. I had two or three hours with Tony Caro yesterday – who you may remember is one of the artists I have spent most time over the years talking and arguing with – and although I don't agree with some of his commitment he is one of the very few people I know who has as much, or more, vitality and mental energy towards art as I feel I have. Not that these are the *sine-qua-non* of good art – but they help. I want my next show to be a very strong one – like nailing my colours to the mast and forcing people to look again and not just take me for granted as another 60s 'cool' painter still doing his thing!'

The letter is revealing not just about Jeremy's artistic morale. He writes at length about clothes, in which he and Beth had a great interest, boasting of new flared jeans and platform soles. It also offers an insight into how he and Beth are coping with the long-haul demands of parenthood. Jenny, by contrast, is in Pakistan working for the foreign office as a secretary, and in and out of love. 'I can't help being amused by the emotional ups and downs hinted at in your letters which involve being 'on' or 'off'

Pakistan and other continents according to the state of your love life! ... When you first left England you seemed to be feeling very sorry for us stuck in old Kingston! Actually, we've never been in better heart.'

Plans for moving had been put to one side in the face of soaring house inflation and the fact that Jeremy didn't like the idea of living full-time in the country. Perhaps, like J. G. Ballard, he was enjoying the intellectual space of suburbia. He was even playing bridge. 'The children all seem to be far less trouble than they used to be now that they are getting older and although she does have her hands a bit full, Beth is so much happier doing a part-time job. I do a bit more of the routine housework on non-Chelsea days and I don't mind at all.' And while they were hardly wealthy, Jeremy had been selling some paintings. In 1970, for example, he more than doubled his income from teaching at the Chelsea School of Art in this way. 'We are determined not to get any more materialistic and don't really want to anyway.' Instead of moving, he asked an architect friend and neighbour, John Varney, to draw up plans to modify the house a little.

Another reason for his sunny mood is 'the acquisition of a motorbike', his 'agile and quick' Honda 125. 'I use this to go to London (even in the rain) ... I just slip through the gaps at a steady twenty miles-per-hour and get there in twenty minutes.' He was also rediscovering road racing, going to Brands Hatch and Mallory Park to watch, even taking Beth and the children to a race at the circuit in Crystal Palace, nearing the end of its life because of safety concerns. Rob and Ben had loved the experience, so much so that Jeremy had taken Rob and a school friend to Brands Hatch where 'they were so grown up and appreciative that I was absolutely delighted. Needless to say I am not satisfied just watching and long to have a go – but it is sometimes dangerous and obviously if I did some people would disapprove strongly. But I haven't decided not to.'

If Jeremy was happy enough to stay rooted in Kingston, with Rob and Ben at primary school only yards down the road, and their daughter Georgina, born in 1970, now a toddler, heading that way, Beth still had a yearning for wilder landscapes. As a young woman, she and Jenny had hitched up to Scotland on holiday. She was no mountaineer, but she loved the possibility of such places. John Varney, their architect friend, was a Yorkshireman and something of a climber. His two boys were at school with Rob and Ben. They found an advertisement for a cottage at Ravenglass in the Lakes in the back of the paper and almost on a whim booked for both families to share in the spring of 1973. There were walks and a picnic on the Wrynose Pass, where the kids dammed the stream and Ben cut his midriff after diving into the shallow pool they made.

In the mid 1960s, the Moon family had been rather upended by Jack's affair with his secretary. Although a short-lived relationship, it nevertheless ended his marriage to Ruth and Jack married again – to a woman he'd met in Burma during the war. You can sense, in the aftermath, Jack's children drawing together to re-establish family ties. David Moon, who was eight years younger than Jeremy, had started his second job in Richmond in 1969, on the other side of Richmond Park. He would often walk over to see his brother and his wife Beth, and their young family, at the end of the working week. 'For the first time, I got to know him quite well. We had good fun.'

David had joined the family on a camping holiday in the south of France that summer, driving down in convoy and camping on the coast. Then he'd settled back into work at his engineering firm and Jeremy returned to his studio. On the last Friday of November 1973, David phoned his brother's house to invite himself over for supper. A policeman answered. 'He said: "your brother's had an accident. We think he's all right but your sister-in-law's not here. If you're coming over that's good." He genuinely thought Jeremy would be all right. The same policeman had been talking to Jeremy in the ambulance.'

Jeremy, it transpired, had been riding home on his new Kawasaki from his teaching job at the Chelsea School of Art. Nearing Kingston, just after a little humpback bridge but before the Robin Hood roundabout and the exit from the A3 down Kingston Hill, he came off. It's possible he may have skidded on something, like a patch of oil spilt on the road, but whatever the cause, Jeremy found himself sliding away from the bike into oncoming traffic. Always agile, he managed to scramble back into his own lane, where the car he had just overtaken drove over him.

David wasn't too alarmed. It was clearly a serious situation, but from the mood and behaviour of the police, there seemed a strong likelihood that Jeremy would be okay. He had been talking with the police on his way to hospital. Beth was out, leaving Rob to hold the fort, so David promised to come straight round and tell Beth what had happened when she got home. When she returned, Beth put together some things for her husband and she and David drove round to Kingston Hospital. By the time they got there, Jeremy was already dead.

In the back garden, Kingston upon Thames, 1969. **Photo**: Moon Family Collection.

WARDANCE

A parent's sudden death at a young age will inevitably have an impact on their children, but how great an impact is difficult to say. You cannot prove the counter-factual. And so many circumstances enter into the equation – the child's age, background, culture, whether the father or mother has died and the child's own personality – that speculating is dangerous.

Ben was seven when his dad was killed, and Rob was nine, twenty months older than his brother. There is a threshold of understanding between these ages, which might mean Rob's experience of this shattering event was powerfully different to Ben's. Rob certainly has clearer memories of that fateful Friday in November 1973, but Ben, unlike Georgina, who was still a toddler, can still recall its impact.

'I have a few memories,' he says. 'I remember David being around that evening, when we were told he was dead. I remember lying in bed feeling sad. Mum and David were downstairs talking. I remember going to school and feeling different. Special even. Because my dad had died.'

The immediate aftermath of a sudden and premature death has its own momentum and demands. The death of their son brought Jack and Ruth together for the first time since their divorce a few years before. Jack, clever, competitive but prone to depression, must have been particularly vulnerable; he lost a brother, his best man and his son in motoring accidents. But there was a concerted effort to keep control. 'It was a nice funeral,' David says. 'There was a huge turnout. Then the family came up to Cheshire for Christmas. Beth was very good, keeping things on an even keel. The family carried on having meals around the dining table. She continued with how things had been before. It wasn't at all emotional. Very middle class. Stiff upper lip kind of thing.'

The cracks in that armour are glimpsed briefly when the family discusses the inquiry into the crash that killed Jeremy. A witness said the elderly woman driving the car behind had made no attempt to brake. But she left on a cruise soon after the accident and by the time she returned to give evidence to the coroner – several months later – the witness was no longer sure of their initial statement. Before returning an open verdict, the coroner asked the driver if she had anything to say. Just before the accident, she recalled, she had said to her husband, a retired army officer: 'Here comes another bloody fool on a motorbike.'

Ben was left without a complete picture of his father, just fragments and ghosts of memories. 'I can't remember much. I remember him walking me round to the Post Office to put money in my savings account. I remember him getting angry one evening we'd had guests round for dinner and we'd stayed up late. When they left, we went out on to the road. I can't remember what we did, but we were fooling around in some way and he was angry with Rob and me. But then maybe you remember the bad things.'

It's easy to imagine Jeremy, still caught up in his ambitions as an artist, being frustrated at the quotidian demands of young children. Writing to Jenny the year before his death, he mentions visiting his sister Diana at her home in Essex to see her baby son Christopher. 'It's fine,' he writes, 'but I'm glad we're not starting out on babies again – it's a bloody hard grind. Though Beth insists it was all marvellous fun.'

Of course, it would be easy to overstate this. Many fathers, and many mothers too, find early childhood exhausting and even unrewarding. Photographs of Jeremy with his children show that at least some of the time he was relaxed and engaged with his children. In one, Jeremy holds a pole at waist level with Rob and Ben hanging from either end, with Jeremy,

Jeremy and Georgina, 1971. **Photo**: Moon Family Collection.

whose face is out of frame, turning in circles. Ben, in a dead hang from his end of the pole, his short legs lifted off the lawn in the back garden, has a blissful expression on his face, tongue caught between his teeth. In another image, Georgina sits astride her father's neck using his hair for reins, her pram half concealed behind them on the back step.

Ben recalls that his mother never said anything negative about his father. 'She always paints things as positive. But they seemed to have a good relationship and a good family life. I can't imagine how difficult it must have been for her. I think she is an amazing person. To lose your husband and you've got three kids, one of whom is only three. She's a tough character who just got on with it.' Beth would never remarry and although men weren't entirely absent from her life, Ben can only recall two or three, 'and I don't even know how serious that was. I don't think she wanted someone else. She was independent and liked her own company. David was the closest thing we had to a father. Of course, he couldn't be there all the time.'

Whatever impact his father's death may or may not have had on him, Ben is clear about one thing. 'I don't feel like it changed me that much.'

'You were quite a rebellious teenager?'

'Yeah, but I might have been that anyway.'

When reflecting on why people do the things they do, Ben will often offer the idea that they are made that way. Just as he inherited his father's slim build and passion for speed, the implication is that his inherited personality allowed him to cope with the absence of his father. At school and afterwards, his father's death was a fact, not a topic for conversation. He rarely if ever mentioned it to friends and it was never a cause of speculation or self-enquiry. Even now, he says, 'I don't think about what life might have been like very much.' On the other hand, he speaks often of the stability his family gave him. He likes the fact he was born at home, and that his home never moved while he was growing up. It's an attitude he's carried into his own parenthood.

The holidays they'd enjoyed as a family took on a new significance with Jeremy's death, and Beth and David made every effort to recapture some of that joy. In the spring of 1974, they went back to the Lake District with John Varney and his family. It was now that Ben had his first experience of rock climbing. Where exactly is hard to say, but John scouted around Eskdale 'for some bits of rock to take the boys on and found something not too far away at low level.' It wouldn't have amounted to very much, top-roping easy routes on a friendly crag, but the impact it had on Ben was instantaneous. 'Straight away I knew this was what I wanted to do.'

Few of us discover so early in life what puts us in that creative, unself-conscious state of mind variously described as 'flow' or 'the zone'. Ben was lucky. He had an early memory of something that utilised his physical and mental talents and left him fulfilled – something he wanted to experience again and again. Varney later moved back to Yorkshire and bought a farm near Malham in the Yorkshire Dales where he and his family lived a version of *The Good Life*, albeit far from suburbia, with cows, pigs, chickens and ducks. Gradually he developed the farm as a management training centre. Rob and Ben recall a trip to Brimham Rocks, east of Pateley Bridge, but what they did there is lost to memory.

In interviews Ben has often said he began climbing as a seven-year-old, but in reality he began to think of himself as a climber from that age; this handful of childhood climbs was the inciting incident for a lifetime of effort. The difference is important. Young climbers starting at that sort of age can now access training facilities and advice that were undreamed of in the early 1970s. Had Ben grown up near a good climbing wall, by the time he reached his teens the power and particularly stamina that he developed in his adult career would have already been trained. Ben pays little heed to the road not taken; it doesn't serve his interest, so what's the point? Yet the temptation to consider what difference it might have made if he really had started climbing at seven is hard to resist.

If his opportunities to go climbing as a boy were sporadic, the presence of mountains and wilder places in his childhood was more consistent. Despite Jeremy's absence, Beth continued with family holidays in the British hills, spending Easter holidays at a cottage in Dolwyddelan, on the road between Betws-y-Coed and Blaenau Ffestiniog, in Conwy. North of Dolwyddelan is Moel Siabod, the 'shapely hill', highest peak in the Moelwyns, from whose summit you can, at a glance, take in thirteen of the fourteen peaks in North Wales which rise over 3,000 feet. South of the village, above the Lledr valley, is the beautifully situated crag of Carreg Alltrem and its classic route *Lavaredo*.

In his early teens, Beth bought Ben a rope at Ellis Brigham's shop in Betws-y-Coed and he practised on the little crags around Capel Curig. 'She didn't buy me any karabiners though,' he says. 'I had some engineering nuts and a few slings. I remember doing *Hope* on Idwal Slabs with Rob, and putting all the slings on the rope before tying in. If I'd fallen off, the rope would have probably melted straight through them.'

Ben also had a personal and rather unusual connection to the Swiss Alps. His aunt, Beth's sister Margaret, or Meg, had worked for the foreign office in Switzerland, and at a friend's wedding caught the eye of a dairy farmer called Ernest Berruex. He introduced himself, they married, and a couple of summers after Jeremy's death, invited Beth and the children to use a spare chalet at the family farm above Les Diablerets. There was no electricity or running water and the children slept in traditional Alpine beds – essentially wooden boxes – paying for their board by helping out round the farm, quite literally making hay. (Ben's cousin Catherine Berruex, Meg's younger daughter, became a human rights observer for the Temporary International Presence in Hebron. She was murdered in Palestine in 2002, aged just twenty-five.)

These precious childhood experiences of the mountains, the interest of his grandfather that would extend into adulthood and the consequent access to his grandfather's books and personal memories, all formed the culture in which the germ of Ben's climbing life became rooted. As his fame in the climbing world developed, several commentators, thinking they were upholding a great tradition in the face of a soulless gymnast, would berate Ben and his contemporaries for an apparent indifference to the natural world. In Ben's case, the criticism was misplaced. Had you been making predictions about the young Ben Moon's future, you would have assumed him to be a mountaineer in the making, not a future revolutionary who would help change the face of rock climbing.

In his own quiet way, Ben was – is – something of a rebel, certainly antiauthoritarian even if it isn't in his nature to be confontational. But that's not how he approached climbing. When he finally got the opportunity to develop his instinctive interest in the sport, his natural talent and power allowed him to progress with unusual precocity. It wasn't rage against the machine that drove him, or some long-concealed anger prompted by his father's premature death; he responded simply to something he loved doing. The fact that some people would see Ben as a kind of rebel was more to do with historical timing – big changes were already underway when Ben arrived on the scene – and his punkish appearance. Underneath the famous dreadlocks, however, Ben displayed the same shrewd intelligence about how to proceed that his father had in front of a canvas.

But Ben's real start in climbing didn't, however, come from family connections or his experiences on holiday. Like most young men, he would thrive in a small band of like-minded individuals, especially given the position his talent commanded. And it was at school that he would discover this band of brothers.

If it's impossible to know for certain what impact Jeremy's death did or did not have on Ben's character, in the case of his education it was decisive. 'A family friend suggested boarding school to my mother because we didn't have a father. It's quite likely we wouldn't have gone to boarding school otherwise.' The financial implications of that option were far beyond Beth's means, but the Artists' Benevolent Fund wrote to Beth saying they could help in some way. This financial support – and the choice of school – were crucial.

Christ's Hospital emerged from the social turmoil of Henry VIII's dissolution of the monasteries, as the support network offered by the monasteries collapsed and the poor spilled onto the streets. In 1547, the year of his death, the king gave some of the buildings of Greyfriars monastery in Newgate, whose medieval church was the second-largest in London, to the City. Henry's son, Edward VI, inspired by a sermon on caring for the poor given by his bishop of London, Nicholas Ridley, wrote to the mayor encouraging him to act in support of London's destitute, and donated more of his own property to help establish three charitable institutions, one of which was Christ's Hospital. The first pupils were admitted in 1552.

The school's original function – of educating poor children – has been preserved through the centuries, although the purpose of its charitable work is no longer expressed in such stark terms. Fees are now assessed on a parent's ability to pay; it's one of the few private schools that genuinely merit charitable status. (The actor and Christ's Hospital pupil Roger Allam described the school as 'Eton for poor boys'.) Historically, preference has been given to children from an eclectic range of backgrounds, including those born in the parish of Twickenham, which once included Kingston.

Christ's Hospital has survived all manner of upheavals and disasters. The plague of 1665 killed a large number of children, and the Great Fire of London the following year destroyed the school itself, although thankfully without loss of life. It was rebuilt, with contributions from Sir Christopher Wren and Nicholas Hawksmoor. A second royal charter in 1673 established the Royal Mathematics School at Christ's Hospital, funded in part by Samuel Pepys, its curriculum developed by Isaac Newton among others, to produce a supply of navigators for the British ships that were building the empire. In 1902, the school moved, under a cloud of some controversy, to its current site in Horsham, West Sussex.

If the current campus is merely a century old, it has the assured grandeur that is the hallmark of the English public school – sweeping sports fields, handsome buildings and architectural salvage from Wren's contributions to the old site. Christ's Hospital also has the sort of alumni, to set alongside benefactors like Wren and Pepys, that adds irresistible momentum to any institution, particularly its stellar clutch of poets, George Dyer, Samuel Taylor Coleridge (who spent most of his holidays there too), Leigh Hunt, Edmund Blunden and Keith Douglas.

Christ's Hospital is currently divided into eight houses, each in turn split into two. One of these, inevitably, is Coleridge, while another is named for Coleridge's school friend, the essayist Charles Lamb. When Ben arrived at Christ's at the age of eleven to join his brother Rob, he was placed in Maine 'B', named for the nineteenth-century jurist Henry Maine, and when he moved up to the senior school at thirteen, he went into Lamb 'B'. Joining him as a new boy in Maine 'B' was Ric Potter, and the two quickly became close friends. Both would become obsessed with climbing – Potter is now an internationally qualified mountain guide – but their friendship pre-dated their climbing careers so they used what little spare time was afforded them by playing war games in woods near the school and escaping the dreaded hand of authority. 'I have no idea what we talked about before climbing,' he laughs.

There were also strange new customs to absorb, the impenetrable argot public schools use to identify and segregate themselves. Christ's is known as a bluecoat school, after its idiosyncratic Tudor-era school uniform, worn since its first pupils arrived in 1552: belted, long blue coats, knee breeches, yellow socks, and bands, the sort of neckwear worn by Protestant clergy and lawyers. The boys themselves now refer to Christ's as House, and their blue coats as 'housey coats', although not in Ben's day. Even the kind of buckle boys wear on their belts is a signal of age and status. Younger boys wear one of plain leather, but on reaching their Little Erasmus year, when they enter the upper school, they are allowed to wear

Top of the class at Christ's Hospital. **Photo:** Moon Family Collection.

one of sterling silver. 'It was more Harry Potter than Harry Potter,' Ric Potter – no relation – recalls. (The uniform is provided free to all pupils, and remains overwhelmingly popular, judging by a recently rejected offer to replace it with something a little less sixteenth century.)

A raft of ingrained traditions at Christ's come as a consequence of the school's long connection with the City of London. They march in the Lord Mayor's Show and there is an annual parade through the City on St Matthew's Day, while the Lord Mayor attends speech day each summer. The centrepiece of this enthusiasm for parades is the Christ's Hospital Band, founded in the mid-nineteenth century to take the edge off the tedium of the various marches pupils were obliged to make. Not only does it make music, it also performs marching displays, with members crossing in intricate patterns as they march. The band plays every day at school, and performs at various sporting events, including Lord's test matches and rugby internationals.

When Ric and Ben encountered this immense entity marching in blue coats and yellow stockings, saw the excitement and prestige that surrounded it, they saw an opportunity, subconsciously, to lift themselves out of the day-to-day tedium of life in a boarding school where almost every waking moment was scheduled and supervised. At the front of the band, which numbered around a hundred members in the late 1970s, marched two ranks of snare drummers. Watching them march, their eyes were drawn to the drummers, with their extravagant, sweeping gestures as they brought their sticks level with their chins, both of them signed up to learn to drum.

Public schools – and popular culture – have changed a great deal in the last thirty years. In 2005, for example, rock music became part of the curriculum at Christ's when the geriatric heavy metal star Gene Simmons, bass player with the band Kiss, arrived at the school to make a documentary for Channel 4, inculcating ten students in the mysteries of rock, and ultimately preparing them as a support act for Motörhead. The series was inspired, if that's the right word, by the Jack Black film *School of Rock*. What could be more amusing, the producers must have thought, than contrasting a pensioner rock god in spandex and face paint with a bunch of public-school kids dressed like Tudor squires.

It speaks to our cynical and watchful age that pupils blogged about the damage being done to Christ Hospital's brand name, and by extension their own prospects. In the 1970s, kids formed rock groups not to nurture careers in the entertainment industry, but to explode self-serving and outmoded institutions. Self-expression was about remaking the world, not remaking your personal statement. Ben and Ric, like millions of young teenagers, formed their own band, calling themselves the Bash St. Kids. They had one song, The Jam's *'A' Bomb in Wardour Street*. (Paul Weller sang it on *The Old Grey Whistle Test*, chewing gum, dressed in a smart blazer, appearing cadaverous and cross. The lyrics are not his best work – look them up.) The Bash St. Kids had a charismatic lead singer, the actor and Christ's schoolboy Jason Flemyng, the future star of *Lock, Stock and Two Smoking Barrels* and *Snatch*. They held rehearsals in Jeremy's old studio, where his canvases were – are – still stored and where Ben kept his drum kit.

Music was a big part of Ben Moon's young adulthood, ultimately more in helping form his philosophy on life rather than in any practical way, and for alleviating that dismal, grey frustration familiar to anyone who has been incarcerated. 'You got fifteen minutes free time each day,' Ric Potter recalls, 'and you're all in the common room listening to Ian Dury.' In this, Ben found guidance and inspiration from his brother Rob, two years ahead of him at Christ's Hospital. Those with a sibling at boarding school often have a curious relationship with their brother or sister. It is another loyalty, and one that lies outside the all-embracing culture of school, and is therefore sometimes regarded with suspicion. Better to watch out for each other from a distance.

'He looked after me at school,' Ben says. They also climbed together when they were young, and Ben embraced Rob's passion for anti-authoritarian and alternative music. To call it punk might be historically accurate; this was the era of punk, after all. But many people now associate punk with blind rage and excess and little else. Students of *England's Dreaming*, Jon Savage's epic history of the Sex Pistols and their era, know there was a lot more to it than that. But the term punk seems almost too small for the fracturing of old attitudes and beliefs – 'Your mad parade,' as the Pistols termed it – that took place in the late 1970s. Skinheads, anti-fascists, nihilists, eco-activists, utopians, anarchists and radicals tumbled out of this chaos like pepper as Margaret Thatcher ground her way to power.

There was a corner of punk to suit every personality and creed. Rob and by extension Ben were inclined to the more constructive, leftist wing of punk, bands like Crass, self-styled anarchists whose agenda included environmentalism, social housing and animal rights, all wrapped up in punk's signature smash-it-yourself philosophy. (The first Crass gig was in a squat, and ended prematurely when a neighbour cut the power. For anarchists, they could be surprisingly constructive and nuanced, criticising others on the left for inciting violent confrontation with neo-Nazis. Crass' position earned them a withering comparison with the Russian anarcho-communist Peter Kropotkin, who disapproved of the Bolsheviks' violent revolution. That was the 1970s for you.)

Other bands featured in their musical cosmos, like The Damned, early Killing Joke and Flux of Pink Indians, who changed their previous name, the Epileptics, after a complaint from the British Epileptic Association. Their first album – *Strive to Survive Causing the Least Suffering Possible* – charted at No.79. This wasn't so much music as politically inspired happenings with a heavy bass line. Ben's particular favourite was Yeovil group The Mob, whose second album, *Let the Tribe Increase*, is memorialised as a route name for as long as Water-cum-Jolly's Rubicon Wall stands in the Peak District. The Mob was in the orbit of Crass, who had its own label and put out The Mob's first album, but Crass, as the name implies, were from that region of punk that didn't fuss too much with musical competence. The Mob's sound was a little different, blending the psychological introversion of Joy Division with the extra gloom of the band's concern about the likelihood of nuclear war.

Ben was particularly drawn to The Mob's lead singer Mark Wilson, who wore an unruly mop of dyed dreadlocks, and whose personal philosophy is encapsulated in an interview from 2011, recorded just as the band reformed. 'I still like to think we can change the world, that it needs changing, and that it needs radical ideas in order to achieve any of that. Anyone who listens to our music probably feels our ideals better than I can express them in words. It's love and hope and despair and the need to help each other through it all. I know we get a bit of flak for being 'hippies,' but I couldn't give a fuck. We are ourselves and I don't need a label, thanks. That was what being a punk was all about.'

When he eventually left school, Ben developed his own version of

Wilson's hairstyle from a Mohican, like his brother's, that was left floppy and unwashed for too long and evolved into dreadlocks. In doing so, he offered an image of himself to the climbing world as punkish and alternative, an impression his low profile did nothing to explain. He made statements on rock, not in magazines; he changed rules without the need to say why to his critics. Ben's dreadlocks became part of his identity, a kind of statement in itself, one welcomed by his contemporaries but misunderstood by the climbing establishment.

Yet Wilson's articulation of what The Mob's 'peace punk' was all about offers a more nuanced reflection of Ben's outlook, certainly as a young man, than of someone with no respect for his predecessors in climbing or a selfish disregard for the feelings of others. There is underlying steel in Ben's personality, but it expresses itself more in how he approaches what he does and not in how he relates to others. Those who know him consistently characterise Ben as likeable and trustworthy, concerned for others, steady and loyal. And as Ric Potter says: 'He seems now very much as he was then.'

There were a lot of Londoners at Christ's Hospital, quite a few of them energised by punk, especially The Clash. Dubbed 'the thinking-man's yobs' by the NME for their stridently left-wing agenda, The Clash had a loyal following in many of England's public schools where oppressive nineteenth-century regimes were finally giving up the ghost. There was no privacy at Christ's Hospital, no curtains on the windows and the slipper awaited those who crossed apparently arbitrary lines of control.

Ben did not face this limitation on his freedom head on, although as Ric recalls, he developed more of an attitude later in his school career, partly under his brother's influence when Rob returned to Christ's after his A-levels sporting a dyed Mohican. Potter recalls looking at Rob thinking: 'Yes, you've definitely left school.' But apart from smoking behind the bike sheds and the occasional drinking session, Ben wasn't badly behaved, despite the restrictions and lack of privacy.

Unlike today, there were no girls at Christ's. The school had begun as co-educational and became progressively more segregated until the sexes were educated at different sites. The girls moved to Horsham in 1985, years after Ben had left. 'It didn't bother me at the time,' Ben says. 'It was just how things were. But when you get out of school you do feel that you're less able to communicate with women because you haven't been around them. Maybe I'd have been like that anyway, but I was quite shy.'

Perhaps if he had been more academic then Ben would have got on better at school. 'I wasn't unhappy,' he says. 'I just didn't want to be there. I didn't want to study. I was initially okay, from eleven to thirteen. I worked hard and made an effort. But when climbing came along I became distracted. I had been struggling in lessons and because climbing came so naturally to me, I wanted to do that instead.' According to Ric Potter, 'you were made to feel that if you didn't get good grades your life would be a waste. It was that sort of place.'

There are countless stories of talented, successful people who didn't fit in at school because they weren't suited to its teaching structure or emphasis but who flourished when they found what inspired them. Ben might not have pursued drumming, but Mick Fleetwood found it to be his route out from an academic world that made no sense to him. An even better example is the dancer and choreographer Gillian Lynne, whose mother was so concerned by the negative reports she was getting at school that she took her daughter to see a psychologist.

After talking with her, and hearing about her inability to sit still – a 'symptom' that might get a child a prescription for Ritalin these days – the doctor put on some music and told Lynne that he needed to step out to talk to her mother for a few minutes. He and Lynne's mother then watched through a window as she leapt off her chair and began moving round the room in time to the music. The psychologist recommended a dance school as a course of treatment. Gillian Lynne danced her first major solo in *Sleeping Beauty* at Sadler's Wells on the day she turned twenty.

Climbing would prove to be Ben's escape, and in the same way that Mick Fleetwood and Gillian Lynne could talk about music and dance as being easy and pleasurable, so Ben describes discovering rock climbing. The pleasure and excitement of being young and in love with what you're doing still energises him. He had the great fortune of finding what he was good at and took pleasure in his ability and the sense of purpose it gave him. 'The minute he got into climbing,' Ric Potter says, 'he was completely obsessed with it. Perhaps it was because he was so good.'

The switch was thrown during their first summer in the upper school, when they were thirteen years old. Both arrived for the summer term fresh from climbing over the Easter holidays and when they shared what they'd been doing, both realised they had a new passion in common. Now Christ's began to work in Ben's favour. Two masters, Andrew Gunning and Clive Kemp, organised an afternoon's rock climbing on Monday afternoons. Gunning was more of a mountaineer; Kemp was a keen skier who taught Latin. Both teachers were well liked, Kemp's sudden and premature death in 2004 prompting memories from former pupils of his kindness and quiet support.

A minibus would leave Christ's after lunch with whoever wanted to come along. Its usual destination was Bowles Rocks, a few miles south of Tunbridge Wells, across the border from Kent in East Sussex, and an hour's drive from Horsham, on the other side of East Grinstead. It is one of the jewels of sandstone climbing in the south-east of England, a former wartime shooting range and pig farm rescued from obscurity in the 1960s by John Walters to become a climbing gymnasium for rock-starved Londoners. It's now a successful outdoor centre. 'As a young teenager, I just loved it,' Ben says. 'You walk up the road and the cliff's right there. I think it had a good impact on me. It's technical and hard – and pretty much bouldering. It gave me some power and was good for my technique.'

In 1980 there were few climbing walls in the country as a whole, let alone

Ben climbing *Hate* at Bowles Rocks. **Photo: Ben Moon Collection.**

in Sussex, and so beyond those Monday afternoon excursions, Ben and Ric had to improvise. There was a familiar half-built structure on the playing fields dubbed the 'Magic Mountain' that had in fact been conceived as an artificial climbing wall and had chunks of brick sticking out of it as edges for hands and feet. There was also a sandstone railway bridge they could train on near the school.

Suddenly Ben found himself at the heart of a small but dedicated clique of perhaps half a dozen climbers who would meet up in the holidays on the same sandstone crags. Suddenly, nothing was remotely as important as climbing. Ben's one small area of private space at school was his desk with an area of wall above it that he could fill with posters, not with pictures of punk bands but posters from *Crags* magazine, of his hero Ron Fawcett climbing North Wales routes like *Right Wall* at Dinas Cromlech and *Citadel* at Gogarth. He choose climbing as the topic for a school project, which prompted him to write to his grandfather for his memories of climbing in the 1930s. He pored over Alan Blackshaw's classic instructional work *Mountaineering*.

'He was easily the best climber,' Potter says. He remembers 'messing around on harder Bowles routes like *Hate* and *Digitalis*,' both hard, technical problems, certainly for schoolboys in the early 1980s, 'and then Ben just did them. All those pull-ups were paying off.' Suddenly the quiet, self-possessed teenage boy was the focus of attention among his peers. 'He was the best,' Potter says. 'Immediately, he was the man. When you're in that situation people defer to you a bit, and that makes you more confident. You're going to enjoy it. But mostly I remember him being really keen.'

By 1981, Ben was desperate to climb further afield on some of the crags more commonly featured in the magazines he pored over. To their northern perspective, places like Bowles were almost foreign curiosities, worth only sporadic attention. So in September, Ben wrote a cogent letter to his grandfather, asking him if he could come and stay with him in Cheshire to go climbing at Lawrencefield after Christmas.

Jack sent him back an encouraging letter, with observations about the short days and his ignorance of Lawrencefield, a gritstone quarry considerably further away than some of the excellent edges in Staffordshire, like the Roaches, which would have been a more logical target. A teenager with a smartphone can now book a climbing holiday on an obscure Greek island in about five minutes. Then, it took longer, and wrong turns were easily made.

After thinking about it, Jack wrote his grandson a second letter, giving sound reasons why a climbing trip was difficult – lack of light, the exigencies of quarry climbing – and having talked it over with his Uncle David concluded it wasn't on. 'I am not trying – or wanting – to put you off climbing. It is a wonderful pastime and I only wish I had started at your age. You have plenty of time in front of you, so don't risk making a wrong move in your natural enthusiasm.'

Jack's sympathy for his grandson's near desperation to get to the crags did prompt him to add: 'I should like to have a chat with you about climbing, and we could look at a few photographs and books. You can keep those I sent you and have anything else which might interest you.'

The following Easter, before Ben turned sixteen and sat his O-levels, he and Ric finally did get away, catching a bus to North Wales from Victoria for their first climbing trip outside the south-east. They got off in the Ogwen valley and spent the week camping and hitching around the famous climbing grounds of Snowdonia in poor weather. Their first routes were on Little Tryfan and then *Grooved Arête* on Tryfan's east face, one of the great examples of early rock-climbing exploration, and just the kind of route to thrill his grandfather. It was the first time either of them had led anything, since Bowles is strictly a top-roping and soloing venue.

Considering themselves suitably experienced, they decamped to the Llanberis Pass to climb on the famous open-book walls of Dinas Cromlech. Their choice of routes was unusual. Most climbers are drawn first to the perfect clean walls of the Cromlech's central feature, but Ric and Ben climbed on the crag's west wing, selecting an obscure route called *Speedfreak*, which starts up an arête, then quite loose, with little protection above a sharp flake. Ben cruised up this as easily as he had the routes in Ogwen, begging the question of why he hadn't tackled more famous challenges – like *Cemetery Gates* or *Cenotaph Corner*. Although given what happened next, it's possible they thought they were on another route.

Dinas Cromlech's east wing has notoriously loose and vegetated rock. For example, *Sexton's Route*, as described in Paul Williams' guidebook, is 'a must for the amateur botanist who detests crowds'. *Horseman's Route* is 'a rambling expedition with its share of bad rock and vegetation which is somewhat redeemed by its imposing final chimney.' *Horseman's* was probably what Ben and Ric were after, and which they failed to find, ending up instead on a line to the right of *Jericho Wall*, rock previously left unclimbed for good reason. Even the mythically enthusiastic Paul Williams could find nothing positive to say about Ben Moon's first new climb when he wrote it up: 'A poor route on doubtful rock.'

Once they realised their error, Ben and Ric wrote a description of their creation and sent it to Pete Livesey, a revolutionary punk himself, after a fashion, then writing a column about latest developments for *Climber* magazine. They called it *Wardance*, at Rob's suggestion, after a track on Killing Joke's first album, a suitably apocalyptic cultural reference. 'I don't suppose anybody's done it since,' Ric Potter says.

They hitched back to Capel Curig to catch the bus home, intending to sleep in the public toilets, 'but when we got there Ellis Brigham had a tent sale on, and had put the tents up in a field, so we slept in one of those.' Their first trip away had been a huge success for two fifteen-year-olds who didn't yet have a firm grip of what they could do. At Victoria bus station Beth met them off the coach with the news that the country was at war and a fleet was on its way to the Falkland Islands. A few weeks later, as British troops fought their way to Port Stanley, Ben took his O-levels. His grandfather wrote to him, commenting on the devastating loss on

Everest of two of Britain's finest mountaineers: 'A miserable business about [Joe] Tasker and [Pete] Boardman. I don't suppose it will ever be known how near the summit they got.' Ben, however, was focused on a more personal milestone – his first alpine season.

Christ's Hospital's trip to the Alps was the brainchild of their teachers Andrew Gunning and Clive Kemp and a brilliant opportunity for both Ric and Ben. ('Ric and I are at the top,' he wrote in a letter home, 'and are probably the most senior to Mr Gunning, so we get on all the trips and organise things. How about that?!') Climbing in the mountains was still Ben's ultimate aim. He saw himself as an all-round climber following in his grandfather's footsteps. Boys and masters went first to Leysin in Switzerland to do some mountain walking and build fitness. 'Yesterday we climbed Pic Chaussy and I looked down on Brison [his Aunt Meg's house],' he wrote in a postcard home. 'I could just about see Meg's house. Nightlife's about non-existent, beer's not too expensive.'

After that the party moved on to Chamonix to learn ice-climbing techniques; Ben dressed in a tartan shirt, woollen breeches and old-style, strap-on crampons. Now prepared for anything, the Christ's team moved back to Switzerland and the Arolla valley, climbing a number of classic routes, including the Pigne d'Arolla from the Vignettes hut, an easy, two-hour snow climb, and a rock route on the Aiguille de la Tsa, both peaks over 3,500 metres in altitude. Ric's photographs of Ben on the summit of the Pigne show him squinting into the bright sunshine. He seems younger than sixteen, but equally he looks comfortable, at ease with his surroundings. Decades later, Ben would suggest to Ric that they do some mountaineering together: 'It's what I meant to do, before I got sidetracked into rock climbing.'

Back from the Alps, Ben collected his O-level results. Much as he expected, they weren't good enough for him to continue at Christ's Hospital; they didn't see much point in him coming back to try again. School was out – forever.

The Railton Road flat scene in Brixton. **Photo**: Ben Moon Collection.

THE MOB

Home from the Alps, and without the necessary grades to continue at Christ's Hospital, Ben enrolled at a local college to do A-levels, but he made no serious or sustained effort to turn his academic career around. He was living at home again with his mother and Georgina. 'Mum didn't seem worried but it's possible she didn't know what I was doing. I bunked off a lot from college and spent a lot of time in my father's studio.'

Where before he had played drums and rehearsed Jam covers with future Hollywood actors, now he trained for climbing. There was an old sofa in the studio and a record player and a little tape recorder belting out Toto's *Africa*. He had a collection of climbing magazines to pore over and started cutting up the unused stretchers for his father's canvases and hammering them to the wall with masonry nails to give narrow edges fifteen millimetres wide on which he could traverse backwards and forwards. He also built a kind of proto-campus board and while his classmates were doing double physics, Ben was working instead on his finger strength.

'The studio was my den,' he says. 'I spent a lot of time there that winter, planning to get away.' His chosen destination was Freÿr in the Belgian province of Namur, rather forgotten now and certainly less inspiring than crags further south but in the early 1980s one of the new continental limestone destinations that were drawing increasing numbers of British climbers and were the subject of magazine articles. 'I figured out I could get a job in a restaurant and climb all day.'

This was quite enterprising for a sixteen-year-old, but while he dreamed of the future in his father's studio his connection to education was weakening further. Eventually he stopped going to college altogether and got a job stacking shelves for a chain of pharmacies. As spring turned to summer, he caught the train on his days off to Eridge, continuing on foot to Bowles. His *Southern Sandstone* guidebook shows a tick against almost every route, most of them dated from this period. There's a hand-written 'new' climb as well: '*Shuffling Souls* 6b. A direct line up the *Artificial Route*.'[1] *Shuffling Souls* was another track from The Mob.

Not unreasonably, Beth suggested Ben might like to start paying rent, now he was earning and seemed to have given up his studies. Ben was incredulous that he should have to hand over the meagre rewards from such a boring occupation. So he quit. He also announced he was moving out; careful research at the Department of Health and Social Security into his rights revealed he would be entitled to the dole and housing benefit if he did so.

Looking back, his next step was daring and romantic, but at the time made some of his friends and family uneasy. With Lewis Horsman, another old school friend who had also flunked his O-levels, Ben moved to Brixton and a flat in Railton Road, where Brixton's riots had started two years before. The fuel for the riots was racial prejudice, exemplified by the 'sus' laws – police powers to stop and search that were dispropor-tionately used against London's black community – as well as the twin scourges of unemployment and poor housing.

Not a huge amount had changed when Ben and Lewis moved into their flat. 'It was very run down. Our landlord lived downstairs and we shared a kitchen. We often saw him around.' It was hot that summer, and the windows were usually open. 'There were people on the street all the time, it was good fun, and a great place to go gigging.' It was in Brixton that his Mohican

---

1 Ben later discovered he had done the second ascent of this line, after Matt Saunders.

began to evolve – in the absence of regular showers – into dreadlocks. 'During the day we'd go to parks and hang out and drink cider.' Ric Potter, now studying for A-levels and ultimately a place at university, visited Ben at Railton Road and remembers the flat as a 'shit-hole, a complete dive, a typical DHSS flat.' At one level he was impressed at two sixteen-year-old punks shedding their blue coats and living on their own terms. 'But then you're thinking, what are they going to do? Where will this go?'

If that was the view of an old school friend, you might imagine his mother would have been even more worried. But if Beth had doubts about her son's direction, she kept them to herself. 'She was fine about it,' Ben says. 'She's never been judgmental. She could see I was more or less happy.' Watching a son drift dangerously away from conventional routes to fulfilment might have exasperated or depressed some mothers, but Beth proved calmly supportive throughout Ben's career. He has kept a bundle of her letters, mostly written after he moved to Sheffield, none of which pry too deeply into his future plans or lifestyle, but instead are quietly supportive.

Usually she's giving Ben news of what she's reading or been listening to, sending him tapes of Mozart, which he enjoys, or telling him her plans. Ben might have inherited his intense focus from his father, but his calmness, that slight detachment from the minor bumps along life's road, seem more like Beth, the serene mother who held the family together after the wrenching and unexpected death of her husband. As Georgina would write to Ben a few years later: 'Mum's fine. She definitely has the most stable life out of all of us. I'm not sure that's an age thing or more a character thing. She and I definitely regard it as a positive thing.'

Perhaps she simply understood what Ben was like, and that a life hanging round parks drinking cider and going to gigs in grim venues at night wasn't really going to be enough for him. Although he didn't climb much when he was living in Brixton, Ben did manage one trip to the Peak District, a week at Stoney Middleton, dossing, as so many did at that time, in the woodshed at the foot of the crag.

On the Tube, 1982. Photo: Ben Moon Collection.

From the mid 1960s to the early 1980s, Stoney had been a forcing-ground for British rock climbing. It was loved by some and regarded by others as dismal and claustrophobic. As a laboratory for testing the limits of climbing its role can't really be disputed. In going there, Ben was plugging himself more firmly into an arc of climbing history stretching back into the nineteenth century.

From being an activity that was part of a mountaineer's training for the Alps, rock climbing developed as an end in itself towards the end of the 1800s. In 1897 Owen Glynne Jones – myopic, scientifically gifted, self-absorbed and hungry for fame – climbed *Kern Knotts Crack*, a contender as the first route to be graded Very Severe. To do so, he first climbed the route with a top rope, cutting out the risk so he could practise the moves. This earned him the scorn of his contemporaries including the notorious diabolist and early climber Aleister Crowley: '[Jones] used to go out with a couple of photographers and have himself lowered up and down climbs repeatedly until he had learned its peculiarities, and then make the 'first ascent' before a crowd of admirers.'

Crowley is describing a method modern climbers would call 'headpointing'; practising moves in safety before leading them with all the attendant risks but with the knowledge that you could physically do the moves. Jones was modern in another respect; he liked attention and saw the crags as a stage on which to perform. The 'couple of photographers' Crowley mentions were the Abraham brothers, the most successful early climbing photographers. In combining forces, the three of them created an unstoppable publicity machine. The correlation with the modern climbing scene is quite startling.

Physically strong, Jones was not a natural climber; George Abraham described him as 'rough and spasmodic'. But he was ferociously determined. Choose almost any period in the history of rock climbing and you will find someone like him with similar drive, for example Pete Crew in the 1960s and someone else whose motivation and skills are different – like Martin Boysen. Ethical concerns ebb and flow as each succeeding generation tries to make its mark; different aspects of climbing appeal to different types of personality. Rock types come in and out of fashion; crags are worked out and new ones become fashionable.

Following that arc to Ben's appearance on it, two things changed in predictable ways: routes got harder and climbing equipment got better. In fact, the two fed off each other. As ropes got stronger and more reliable and protection improved, climbers were able to press on with a greater safety margin and try harder moves on the rock. As the years ticked by, climbing grades rose, like a balloon grazing a building, getting caught and pausing here and there, but breaking free again and lifting inexorably. Much of this progress was achieved against the background noise of ethical debate. Was top-roping allowed? How many pegs should you use on a route? Should you clean a route of its loose rock and vegetation before you tried climbing it?

Most of the improvements in equipment that accompanied this rise in standards were in place by the time Ben came along: nylon ropes protected by a sheath; metal wedges that you could place in cracks of almost any width; camming devices and so forth. The huge improvement in rock-climbing shoes that occurred with the arrival of Firés in the early 1980s was perhaps the last step-change in rock-climbing technology. (It's a different story with mountaineering, where continued developments in fabric technology have made clothing lighter and warmer.)

If improvements in equipment were no longer facilitating a rise in standards, as they had from the days of O. G. Jones, through technological changes provoked by two world wars, to the days of Joe Brown and Don Whillans in the 1950s and their immediate successors, what were the stars of tomorrow to do? Improvements in gear could only take climbing so far. Testing the physical limits of what was possible could only continue if there was some kind of compromise ethically. In a nutshell, most of us climb harder if we don't think we're going to hurt ourselves. Something would have to give.

The solution to this dilemma that emerged as Ben arrived on the scene was the increasing use of expansion bolts, especially on limestone. The old motto that the leader must not fall had been redundant for some time, but the idea that falling was a natural and necessary part of pushing limits became more entrenched. Practising climbs had been regarded as cheating in some way; over the course of the 1980s it became acceptable and as a consequence standards soared. New techniques and new terminology were developed as climbers began to understand not only that you could practise, but which were the best ways of doing it. The consequence of this ethical shift was that grades rose more rapidly than at any other time in climbing's history. This new strand of sport climbing, and later bouldering, now sits alongside the traditional, or 'trad', approach.

Sharing the woodshed at Stoney with Ben was the Australian climber Mike Law. Then in his mid twenties, Law was already a veteran climber, part of a generation that had driven up Australian free-climbing standards throughout the 1970s, a generation that included Malcolm Matheson, Greg Child and Kim Carrigan.

Climbers in Australia were facing the same ethical dilemmas and frustrations as those in Europe. 'In that period,' Law explained in an interview, 'notions of yo-yoing, dogging, frigging, abseil inspecting, working routes, and redpointing hadn't really been understood, classified, or even named. Most of the hard routes weren't really free by the redpoint ethos of today, most routes had aid-placed gear, rests, top-roped sections and so on. But then again we were crap at working routes and made life really hard for ourselves by lowering to the ground each time.'

Law was reaching the end of his full-time climbing career when he met Ben, although he remains an excellent sport climber in his fifties. He moved on to racing Ducati motorbikes and in his thirties went to university, getting a degree and then a doctorate in material science. He has since worked at a nuclear research facility and on redesigning gas pipelines. For Ben, climbing with someone who had appeared in climbing magazines was beyond exciting. 'He'd come all the way from Australia and spent the whole trip at Stoney. At one point he ran out of chalk and asked if he could have some of mine. I had made my own chalk bag out of canvas and a kind of furry lining. But then he said: "What's this? French chalk? You've been using the wrong stuff, mate."'

Ben also met climbers living in Sheffield at Stoney, like Tim Freeman and Ian Jones, known as 'Smeg' and not to be confused with Keith Jones, whose nickname was 'Chipper'. More than a decade before the internet, climbing's social network was found in cheap cafes and pubs at climbing venues around the country, and none were cheaper or more welcoming than the Stoney caff, which had been a focus for Peak District limestone climbers since the 1960s. The crag's mid-level terrace, Windy Ledge, like the woodshed, had been a popular doss for two decades, packed at weekends with climbers sleeping off a session in the Moon, the climber's pub just down the road. During the day, Windy Ledge was, in the 1970s, the equivalent of the Catwalk at Malham Cove in the 1980s, a public stage on which those who thought themselves good enough could perform, climbing Tom Proctor's hardest routes, like *Our Father* or *Circe*. The proximity of British climbing's growing media made Stoney famous, especially to those disconnected from latest developments, which explains in part the presence of climbers like Law who had flown halfway round the world to visit a scruffy disused quarry.

After Jerry Moffatt's first ascent of *Little Plum* in 1981, Stoney's rough and ready allure seemed exhausted and the caravan of rock stars moved on to fresh hunting grounds. Yet if 1970s drinking in pubs was replaced, for the next generation, by 1980s clubbing, the Stoney caff remained a central part of Peak District climbing culture for the next few years. Pretty much every climber who visited the Peak in the mid 1980s could tell you at least some of the graffiti scratched or scrawled on the walls of the caff's perennially damp outside toilets. It was like an insanitary cultural museum. To be there midweek, to be acknowledged by the impoverished but gnarly regulars as someone who could climb, to find a group of like-minded people who saw the value of what he wanted to be, was Ben's idea of heaven. Suddenly he could see his purpose in life. 'It seems like a different world now, with no technology, but it was a fun way to live and a great place to hang out and meet people.'

The climbing, on the other hand, was now elsewhere, as Ben realised from magazine reports and the more involved climbers he was starting to know. So he abandoned the flat in Brixton for good, and caught the bus to Llandudno in North Wales. 'I remember walking up Llandudno's Marine Drive to Pen Trwyn for the first time,' Ben says. 'I remember someone climbing *The Electric cool-Aid Acid Test*, cursing and swearing at Andy Pollitt, saying Andy had sandbagged him.'

The lists of first ascents at Pen Trwyn that summer include routes from some of the biggest names in climbing, Pollitt and Moffatt, Ron Fawcett and

John Redhead. That August, Moffatt made the first ascent of *Masterclass*, a contender for the hardest route in Britain at the time and at 7c+ certainly among the hardest routes in the world. Just as his father put himself at the heart of the contemporary art scene in the early 1960s, so Ben now sought out the hardest climbing scene he could find and set to work. In his memoirs Jerry Moffatt recalled lounging on the back seat pulled from Martin Atkinson's Citröen watching 'a little boy come along the crag. He was a pale-skinned punk rocker, dressed in tight black clothes, wearing colourful bangles, with long dirty black hair. He looked about fourteen.'

Jerry watched as Ben set off up *Axle Attack*, a classic but steep E5 (now graded 7a+) with the crux pulling off a single finger-hold into a steep groove. This Ben managed well enough, but as he carried on up the overhanging wall above, his stamina began to fail. Determined not to give in, especially not with such an impressive audience, he pressed on, as people did in those days, without clipping the bolts. Ben's inevitable fall was consequently huge, and in Jerry's version he comes to rest upside down with those tangled black locks a mere five feet from the ground and a nasty rope burn on one leg. In the filth of Parisella's Cave, where Ben was soon living, this wound turned septic.

It's a good story, and Jerry tells it mostly to Ben's advantage: 'He just kept going and just kept fighting. It is that, above everything else, that gets people to the top.'

Determination and ambition are undoubtedly important in the constitution of a great athlete and without them Ben would have got nowhere in climbing. But it's worth examining a little more deeply Ben's introduction to the man, not yet twenty-one himself, who was then the best climber in the world.

When Ben arrived at Pen Trwyn not long after his seventeenth birthday, his climbing experience was still very limited. The year before, he'd had his week in Wales with Ric Potter, the first time he'd left the south-east, and done his first leads. His hardest climbs were 6a boulder problems on sandstone, useful for *Axle Attack's* crux, but not sufficient for a long, steep route on limestone. He'd acquired whatever stamina he had from training in his father's studio and his brief visit to Stoney Middleton. In choosing to climb *Axle Attack*, he'd moved up three or four grades in one go – and very nearly pulled it off. As Mike Law observed after a lifetime of climbing: 'Most good climbers are bloody strong to begin with, sad but true.' Jerry Moffatt was right to admire Ben's attitude but having the innate power to climb the crux of *Axle Attack* with so little experience was perhaps an even better indication of what was to come. His fingers were – are – naturally strong. He may have dreamt of the mountains, but he was a natural-born rock climber.

That evening Ben went into Llandudno as part of a crowd of dedicated climbers, his fingers raw, his arms tired, his leg injury smarting with pain but utterly content. He had found his tribe. In the pub, someone tried to buy him a drink, but the barman took one look at this innocent-faced tramp and refused to serve him and told him to leave. 'Everyone came out, and Jerry shouted how he'd put a brick through their window. I remember phoning Rob to tell him how I was in Llandudno with Jerry Moffatt.'

In the autumn, as Jerry headed to Germany to stay with Wolfgang Güllich and flash their hardest routes, Ben continued his apprenticeship, climbing *Right Wall* at Dinas Cromlech – with painstaking slowness – before going to Tremadog with Steve Lewis where he 'pretty much ticked the crag, apart from *Strawberries*.' He also left Brixton for good, moving to Sheffield, where he has remained ever since.

Sheffield has always been a focus for climbers, but in the 1980s the scene changed. Mass unemployment and changes in benefits were at least partially responsible for this. You could scrape by on the dole and hitch to crags from Sheffield in a way you couldn't do quite so easily from other cities. Add cheap housing to the mix, and the raw materials for a new and unusual community were in place.

When like-minded people coalesce the chance of creativity and innovation increase. Skint they might have been, but lack of means was no barrier to achievement. Amazing things happened, many of them unconnected to climbing. It was like a ghetto of artists, living out their dreams and making new things along the way. It could also be miserable and bleak. Ben's brother Rob came to study in Sheffield in 1984, by which time Ben was living in a first-floor flat on Southgrove Road. Rob recalled how open everything felt; people would just come and go unannounced. Some people didn't have access to a landline – this was ten years before mobile phones – so the only sure way to find someone was knocking on their door. Other climbing scenes had this communitarian atmosphere, notably Llanberis, but in urban Sheffield it had an edge to it. 'People called round at any time unannounced to hang out,' Rob says. 'I've never come across that in any other city.'

Ben's first Sheffield address saw his name added to the suspect roll call of climbers and others with an 'alternative' lifestyle at a house that has since become infamous – 124 Hunter House Road. Like memorable gigs and football matches, far more people claim to have lived at this notoriously derelict hovel than actually did, but Ben was among them, thanks to an invitation from Tim Freeman, then living there with his girlfriend Mandy.

Tim is one of a handful of outstanding but obscure climbers from the 1980s whose names prompt respect from those better known to the climbing public. Stevie Haston once described him as 'lighter than helium.' Ben himself says, 'Tim was really strong, as strong as anyone, and really clever.' Living at Hunter House Road immediately put him in the centre of an intensely active climbing scene, punkish, argumentative, competitive and verging on revolutionary, either in terms of climbing, or politics, or both. Also living at Hunter House Road was Zoe Brown, the pink-haired, ear-studded daughter of arguably the greatest British rock climber of the twentieth century, Joe Brown. Her sister Helen would soon marry Quentin Fisher, one of the best climbers in this new Sheffield scene and an extravagant party-goer.

Zoe was only a few months older than Ben but, having grown up in a 1970s North Wales climbing scene famous for the ambition and scope of its decadence, was a little more worldly wise. She was living at 124 Hunter House Road when Ben arrived, recalling it as 'indescribably bad. The back door wouldn't open, but the doorframe itself would come out of the wall. So at the start of summer we'd take the whole door set out and prop it up in the back garden and leave it there until the weather got cold again.' There was garbage and dirty plates everywhere, most especially on the floor, drugs paraphernalia and more evidence of what the legal system likes to call a 'chaotic lifestyle'. During the winter, they pulled the linoleum up from the kitchen floor and used it to go sledging on the outskirts of the city.

At Zoe's suggestion, she and Ben made plans to visit Fontainebleau at the end of the year, saving the necessary funds from their dole by living on lentils and the generosity of their housemates. ('I remember the gang gave us some cash,' she says.) Ben even had enough scraped together for a pair of the revolutionary new Boreal Firé rock boots that had arrived in Britain that summer. Since they were both under eighteen, and Mrs Thatcher's government had in 1980 somewhat cynically re-classified sixteen and seventeen-year-olds as children, Zoe and Ben were getting just £15.80 a week in supplementary benefit, rising to £16.50 in November 1983, or around £45 a week in today's money. (If they paid rent, they got housing benefit to cover it, as did others who lived there, prompting an inspection by a Sheffield City Council housing officer in the spring of 1984, when 124 Hunter House Road was declared unfit for human habitation and rapidly boarded up.)

It's hard to imagine a more romantic notion than two seventeen-year-old waifs catching the bus to Paris, although both insist their relationship was platonic. Ben says he spoke better French then than he does now, thanks to a solid grounding at his primary school in Kingston. They experienced a series of curious mishaps before Paris – a wheel flying off, customs officials filling the bus after finding 'a suspicious white powder in a young woman's luggage' – before they were spat out at Fontainebleau, taking up residence under a boulder at Bas Cuvier, where they spent the nights shivering and being terrified by nocturnal sounds and visitors.

Jerry Moffatt had been to Fontainebleau that autumn, getting local knowledge after bumping into Parisian climbers Marc and Antoine Le Menestrel, so was able to point Zoe and Ben in the right direction. This was vital information, not just in an era before personal computers let alone the internet, but also because bouldering was an activity of only passing interest to many British climbers and consequently not properly covered in climbing magazines. Now, as Ben puts it, 'It's not only that everyone knows everywhere immediately, it's not just that you know the problems – you know where the holds are.'

Fontainebleau soon became and remains one of Ben's favourite places to climb. 'I remember walking around and thinking: "I really like this."' The rock – a form of sandstone – was similar but better than the crags he'd grown up with in the south-east of England. But if the bouldering was outstanding, it was as much the natural surroundings and atmosphere that inspired him, the wildness of the forest and the light filtering through the trees. Apart from a few gritstone crags in the Peak District, Fontainebleau is the place he has climbed at most consistently throughout his climbing life.

Almost out of cash after a week, their journey home turned into a protracted nightmare. A national holiday meant the buses were full and they were forced to spend the night in Paris. Looking for somewhere cheap in a dodgy neighbourhood, they were kerb-crawled by a car full of aggressive-looking locals demanding to know what they were doing. 'We nearly crapped ourselves,' Zoe says. 'By complete chance we met an English teacher who put us up for the night.' At the bus station, in the way of seventeen-year-olds, Ben and Zoe momentarily wandered away from their rucksacks and discovered them gone when they returned. Rushing outside,

Ben saw a tramp stepping cautiously in the strange, smooth-soled boots he'd found in Ben's rucksack. 'I tell you, no one but a tramp would steal our luggage. We weren't much more than tramps ourselves.'

That winter, while his old school-friend Ric Potter was studying for his A-levels, Ben spent a lot of time training with Jerry Moffatt. 'Why me? That's a good question. He saw that I had talent, but Jerry being Jerry, you wouldn't think he'd show me the tricks of the trade. Maybe it's because I was around and keen, and he couldn't find anyone else.'

Ben and Jerry were the two leading British sport climbers of the late 1980s, setting standards not just in the UK but around the world too. Their era marked a sea change in rock climbing, a staggering rise in standards prompted by a deep shift in the sport's ethical framework. Their names are often linked together, but while they remain good friends, and climbed together often, their careers spanned slightly different periods; as Ben, Jerry's junior by a little more than three years, came into his full strength, they spent less time in each other's company, especially at the crag. 'There was a period when we were competing with each other and didn't climb together.' They both loved rock climbing for the pleasure it gave them, but their motivation to train and work hard at it differed profoundly. 'I've had some great times climbing with Jerry,' Ben says. 'He's got a lot of energy and that's infectious. You feed off that. And he's entertaining, a good laugh.'

Moffatt had emerged in 1980 with a flawed but widely publicised ascent of Ron Fawcett's *Strawberries* and the kind of public profile that earned him comparisons with the tennis star John McEnroe, then at the height of his fame. 'Jerry wasn't a hero of mine,' Ben says with a grin. 'Ron was my hero. Jerry was the upstart.' In fact, Jerry acted as a bridge between the world Ron epitomised and a future of soaring technical standards and specialisation. His achievements spanned several disciplines in sequence: traditional free climbing, highlighted by his ascent of *Master's Wall* in 1983; sport climbing; competitions and bouldering.

Ben speaks fondly of trips they took together to various parts of the world, and is grateful for the help that Moffatt gave him along the way. But he also found that Moffatt's intensely competitive nature got in the way sometimes. 'He had me in a headlock in Tokyo,' Ben says. The two of them had been invited to Japan for a climbing competition and at the time were heavily into car-driving video games. 'They had amazing games in Tokyo, things we'd never seen before in England. Basically, he pushed me off the track to win. I said to him, what are you doing? That's cheating. I had a go at him for that. He got angry and grabbed me.'

It's no coincidence that this unlikely scene, with two of the world's leading climbers grappling over a video game, played out during Moffatt's most intense period of competition climbing. In his memoirs, Moffatt explains his decision to quit the circuit as wanting 'to get myself back again.' It seems the stress of competition can do that – even to someone who revelled in it as much as Moffatt. Both men had been at an event in Austria shortly before Japan and Moffatt had been the runner-up. 'He said he was pissed off at me, because he'd come second there and I hadn't congratulated him,' Ben says. 'And I hadn't because I thought he'd be disappointed.'

Superficially they had quite a lot in common: both privately educated, albeit under very different circumstances and in very different schools, and both utterly dedicated to climbing. Like Johnny Dawes, the other exceptional rock climber from this period, they also shared a passion for motor sport and were audibly southerners in a sport full of northern accents, a fact that grated with some. They also shared a willingness to learn; that was what Jerry admired in Ben from the start. But their personalities were very different. 'Jerry liked to be the centre of attention; he's a great story-teller,' Ben says. 'I'm quite quiet. Jerry likes being well known.' Does he? 'No, not really. It's nice to be appreciated for the things you do. Otherwise I'm not bothered.'

Their different personalities were expressed in their different approaches to climbing. Although he spent a brief period sport climbing, Johnny's

fluid and mercurial climbing style and his fascination with the psychological demands of traditional climbing meant he followed a very
different path to Jerry and Ben – although they all shared a passion
for bouldering. Performance, training, benchmarks – these were not
Johnny's style. Jerry on the other hand made a point of hunting down the
hardest routes of his rivals. He found it intolerable to be around other
climbers when he was injured and couldn't compete. It was reflected in
his ferocious tenacity on the rock, never giving up on a route, doing
whatever he could to stay on the rock no matter how sketchy he looked.
Ben's interest was more abstract. He wanted to climb the hardest
sequence of moves a human being could and would ultimately bend his
focus exclusively to that end. His style was smoother, more controlled,
but he was no less of a fighter. He was just less extrovert about it.

Moffatt had travelled extensively in the US in 1982 and early 1983,
repeating many of America's hardest routes. He spent time with top
American climber John Bachar who was taking a far more scientific
approach to training than any of Moffatt's contemporaries in the UK,
albeit blended with some Californian hocus-pocus. Bachar scrutinised
every aspect of training – diet, psychology, stamina and power. He showed
Moffatt his training area at Joshua Tree in California – dubbed Gunsmoke
– and taught Moffatt how to use the roped stepladder he developed as
a training aid.

'Jerry had just spent a lot of time with Bachar and would say himself he
learned a lot from John. I picked up a lot of that. Jerry was very patient
with me. He was three years older and a much better climber, and already
known around the world. So we went where he wanted to go. It was his
agenda. That didn't bother me at the time, although I wouldn't have done
it later. But there was always a route for me to do.'

Preparing for their spring campaign in France, Jerry and Ben would
hitch out to Stoney Middleton where they top-roped routes for stamina
and Jerry set up his Bachar ladder. They worked difficult sequences on

Broomgrove Road. **Photo:** Jerry Moffatt.

one of the Sheffield Polytechnic buildings on the Collegiate Crescent campus, within walking distance of Hunter House Road. Or else they were in the Polytechnic gym, which would later have a rudimentary climbing wall, but in those days was simply a place to pump weights and do pull-ups. 'We did a lot of dead-hanging as well,' Ben says. 'If anyone asks me now what to do with their training, I tell them dead-hanging and pull-ups.'

In March, Ben and Jerry hitched from Sheffield to Fontainebleau, and after a couple of days suffering through cold nights bivouacked under the boulders, they moved on to Le Saussois, a hundred miles further south. It's something of a backwater now, but this impressive and beautiful crag of limestone buttresses and towers above the Yonne river was one of the crucibles of French sport climbing in the 1980s. Ben and Jerry were there because of Jean-Pierre Bouvier's route *Chimpanzodrome*, at one time the hardest route in France, which had stopped a strong British team including Andy Pollitt and Ron Fawcett not long after its first ascent. It was Jerry's plan to climb this 7c+ first go.

When they got there, dossing in a cave at the crag and walking an hour each morning to a local boulangerie for bread, they discovered that Marc Le Menestrel, climbing with his brother Antoine, had added an even harder route, France's first 8a+, just to the right of *Chimpanzodrome* – called *Le Bidule*. So Jerry began working this, still using what was called yo-yo style, climbing to a high point, falling off, lowering to the ground and then trying again, essentially with a top-rope to his highest piece of protection. While he attempted *Le Bidule*, Ben concentrated on *Chimpanzodrome*.

'He was miles better than me,' Ben says. 'And I didn't have any idea about the climbing there, whereas Jerry had a tick-list of routes to do. I was just going climbing. I didn't have a plan. But because I was climbing all the time, I was getting better really quickly.' In the three days Jerry spent working and then successfully climbing *Le Bidule*, Ben completed *Chimpanzadrome*. His previous hardest grade had been 7a+ at Pen Trwyn the year before. As an indication of raw talent, his ability to skip grades and progress almost to the limit of what was then being done marked Ben out. Marc Le Menestrel was an even greater prodigy, climbing his first new 8a, *Rêve de Papillon*, at Buoux in 1983, when he was just fifteen. ('I have to work very hard to be modest,' he once joked.) Precocious ability was nothing new, but with the arrival of climbing walls from the 1980s onwards – and soon after a youth competition circuit – it has become much more common.

On Jerry's twenty-first birthday, which fell happily on a Sunday so Le Saussois was busy with admiring fans, he flashed *Chimpanzodrome*. Then he and Ben, after routinely despatching *L'Ange*, France's first 7b, levelled their thumbs at the Autoroute du Soleil with the aim of reaching Buoux in Provence. Jerry had been there in late summer the previous year for a photoshoot, and although it had been too hot to climb, he had been impressed. At Le Saussois, Ben recalls, local climbers had told them about the new wave of climbs being done at Buoux. It was impossible to resist the call.

After a night out sleeping at the péage, they gave in and caught the train south, Ben eating into his tiny cash reserves. 'I had absolutely no money,' he recalls. 'I was often hungry. I remember walking round Apt and looking in bakery windows at patisseries, and thinking how I would love to be able to afford something. But it was all too expensive.'

He recalls being cold at night, despite the arrival of spring, perhaps because he wasn't eating enough. 'We were dossing under the bridge in Apt, and I remember being woken by some guy with a really fierce Alsatian. Dossing in public places is just what you did. I was at a trade fair in Salt Lake City recently and flew home via Los Angeles. The flight got in at midnight and left at seven next morning, so I thought I'd just doss out. It's what I used to do all the time. I found a patch of grass just outside the airport and then realised I'd got too old.'

Hitching to the crag proved horribly time-consuming. 'It took five hours one day.' But one morning they got a lift with a young woman who worked in the Auberge des Seguins underneath the crags. 'She was so unbelievably kind,' Ben says. 'She told us about this little cabin behind the auberge that we could use for free. We stayed there for three weeks. She'd get us bread in the morning, and since we didn't have a stove, we ate sandwiches. Banana and Nutella, twice a day.' They also drank water from the local stream, until Jerry got ill and spent three days curled up in his sleeping bag. He'd left the camping stove behind in Sheffield to make room for his Bachar ladder, so he could keep up with his training regime. Ben hitched into Apt and bought a cheap stove and some soup. 'Jerry always said that soup was the best thing ever.'

Buoux is a beautiful place to go climbing. The rock is a combination of sandstone and limestone, a result of the immense geological upheaval that formed the Alps, and the combination of colours, from golden, earthy tones to blue, is sublime. Dramatic buttresses up to 300 feet high sit on the northern side of the Aiguebrun valley, a region of oak forests and truffles, and plantations of lavender. The rock, soft enough to weather into cave systems and so inhabited in prehistory, is pocketed, and the climbing is consequently rather precise, on steep ground and hugely powerful off sharp deep holes.

Jerry was concentrating on the new climbs of around 8a+ being done at Buoux by the Le Menestrel brothers and Jibé Tribout, like *Rêve de Papillon* and *Elixir de Violence*, and doing the previous generation of routes, where possible, on sight. Ben recalls his limit as around 7c. 'I spent six days on a route called *Fissure Serge* on Bout du Monde, close to more famous routes like *Chouca* and *La Rose et le Vampire*. It's 7c+. I remember a long dyno to a pocket. I spent five days falling off that move. Jerry did it in a day. He was doing training laps on it while I was trying to finish it. Eventually I gave up and we went to Verdon.' The route is now rated 8a, at a crag that is notoriously mean with its grades.

Despite the frustration, it's fair to say that Ben had fallen for Buoux. No other British climber formed quite the same relationship with this cliff as Ben Moon; he would spend months of his life working on the world's hardest routes, including his own. 'When we first arrived there was hardly anyone there. I just loved it. It really suited me. Steep, powerful, with pockets and not too technical. It was better bolted than anything in Britain at that stage, but there were still some long run-outs.'

'Did you feel lacking in technical ability then?'

'I've got a reasonable technique but at that stage it wasn't one of my strong points. People would take the piss out of me for it – and for my footwork. It improved a lot though.' Along with his formidably strong fingers, Ben also had immense natural strength in his lower back, able to lift his hips and legs to make the most of footholds. But in so many ways, like many climbers in this experimental era, they were ignorant of how to treat their bodies to get the best results. 'In 1984, when Jerry and I went to France together, we didn't even warm up on easy routes. We picked the climb we wanted to do and just got on it. We'd have been sleeping rough the night before. We'd be cold and even hungry.'

'How can you perform when you're struggling to get to the crag?'

'I don't even remember thinking about that. I just got on with it.'

The contrast with the top French climbers putting up the routes they were trying taught both men a great deal. 'Jibé Tribout was super-motivated,' Ben says. 'He was so tenacious and always tried hard.' Tribout would go on to climb America's first 5.14, *To Bolt or Not to Be*, at Smith Rock, and unlike many of his contemporaries, with the exception of Ben Moon, continued climbing well into middle age. Ben also admired the technical ability of the Le Menestrel brothers, who, like Tribout, had grown up in Paris and became part of the 'Gang des Parisiens' that included Fabrice Guillot and Laurent Jacob. 'If you're climbing a lot at Fontainebleau, you have to be very precise and have very good technique. Southern sandstone is similar.' Marc, six months younger than Ben, was more forceful and determined than his older brother, who was more relaxed and creative in his approach to climbing. It's no coincidence that Marc became a business lecturer and a guru in decision-making while Antoine became an interpretative dancer with his own company, Les Lézards Bleus.

The other strand in French climbing that Ben encountered was from the south. 'With Patrick Edlinger, it was like a show. Everything had to be done perfectly. If you grow up climbing at Les Calanques near Marseille, as Patrick did, you're going to be flowing, more controlled in your movements, because you're not going to meet so many difficult moves. We were a lot more dynamic in style. They used to joke that we always looked like we were about to fall off.'

'A bit slappy?'

'Very slappy.'

Even so, Jerry's ability to climb hard routes on sight, including Antoine's new 7c *Les Caprices d'Anatole*, gave the French climbers something to think about. Antoine later credited him with opening his eyes to what might be possible. Although there was an inevitably competitive edge between the English and French climbers, Ben recalls a lot of warmth too, particularly from Guillot and Jacob. And towards the end of their stay at Buoux, Wolfgang Güllich and a friend with an expensive Mercedes showed up, and took Ben and Jerry out for coffee and a croissant. 'They seemed incredibly wealthy and looked after us a little bit. When Wolfgang saw the rope we were using, a really battered single 9mm, he gave me one of his, a big chunky 11mm.'

Ben and Jerry were soon in the back of the Mercedes, driving east to Verdon, the deep limestone gorge that more than anywhere else epitomised the free-climbing revolution that took place in France in the 1970s. Like every other tourist who drives the winding road along the rim of the canyon, Ben and Jerry peered over the car park balustrade in a state of mild shock. The Verdon river was a turquoise thread 2,000 feet below them, captured by the immense blue and silver walls of the canyon.

Kurt Albert, the father of the redpoint and a close friend of Wolfgang Güllich, arrived from Germany with a vast length of static rope several hundred metres long, and offered to lower Ben and Jerry the height of the gorge so they could climb out again. 'Kurt was so experienced that I didn't think there'd be a problem,' Ben says. 'We both tied on to the end and he lowered us over the edge. We were hanging in space, spinning round like fish, wondering where we'd end up. I don't know what my mum would have done if she'd found out.' When they reached the bottom, almost a thousand feet below, Kurt top-roped them while the two men climbed out simultaneously.

Jerry once again impressed the local climbers with his performances at Verdon, which required a very different style of climbing to Buoux. His ability to overcome the hardest routes on sight put him on the cover of French climbing magazines. He also made the first ascent of a project bolted by Patrick Edlinger, who had in Verdon's recent past made the gorge his own. Called *Papy On Sight*, it became one of Verdon's great classics, so much so that during the 1980s it became polished from the huge number of climbers trying it.

Ben, on the other hand, didn't feel at home climbing at Verdon. 'I didn't like the style of climbing. The friction at Buoux is so much better. Verdon is vertical but technical, and a bit difficult to manage. I still don't know it that well. I was also down to my last pennies. Jerry had money and could go to the cafe with Wolfgang and Kurt but I couldn't afford anything. I had nothing left.'

Exhausted by weeks of continuous climbing, the two English climbers boarded the train home – without tickets.

Strawberries, Tremadog, 1984. **Photo**: Ian Smith.

STATEMENT
OF YOUTH

'I never felt any pressure to conform,' Ben says. 'My family never put any pressure on me to choose a career. I was seventeen, and still really just playing at life, going climbing as often as I could. But if there was a moment when things became more structured it was the spring of 1984 when we came back from France. After we'd seen how the French were doing things, working routes and redpointing them, that's when we got the idea to change our tactics. After France, we started sport climbing. It seemed like the natural thing to do. You could argue that sport climbing in Britain started at this point.'

His first major climb after getting home was Ron Fawcett's 1980 classic *Strawberries* at Tremadog in North Wales. Johnny Woodward had climbed it since Jerry, in the autumn of 1982, and although Ben's ascent offered no improvement in style, it marked another step up in his apprenticeship. He spent a day learning the moves, and because the route is sparsely protected, used the same yo-yo style as the others, leaving his protection but not his rope behind overnight and climbing it first go next morning. 'It felt a bit like redpoint,' Ben says, 'figuring out the climbing and then getting it first off in the morning. It's such an incredible route – aesthetically stunning.' (*Strawberries* got its first on-sight ascent in 1987, from the German climber Stefan Glowacz, then at the height of his considerable powers.)

After *Strawberries*, Ben moved back to Pen Trwyn and Parisella's Cave. 'It was,' he says, 'like sleeping in a dustbowl of sheep shit. If it was nice we slept outside on the grass.' They would eat most frequently at Parisella's Cafe, where the owner, Ben recalls, had a soft spot for that rambunctious enthusiast Paul Williams, an energising force in Welsh climbing and outstanding guidebook writer. 'We were there a lot of the time, and she gave us free food. I was still on the dole, living in Sheffield and I had to go back there to sign on.'

Ben did a lot of routes at Pen Trwyn that summer, not least early repeats of two of Jerry's hardest routes from the previous year, *Oyster* and *Masterclass*. This latter challenge was a fierce direct finish to one of the great routes of the early 1980s, Andy Pollitt's *Disillusioned Screw Machine* – magnificent, sustained and the free-climbing apogee of what had been done at Pen Trwyn at the start of the 1980s, relying on a mixture of bolts and natural gear. *Masterclass* was different, much more technical, much more like where limestone climbing was headed. 'It's bouldery and short,' Ben says, 'but I had a lot of trouble on it because you can't see all the holds. I think I did the third ascent and I couldn't figure it out at all. I remember asking Jerry and he wouldn't tell me. He said I was going to have to work it out for myself. I think eventually he did tell me, because there's a hidden hold.'

Even now, Ben won't be drawn on the grade of *Masterclass*. It teeters on the brink of 8a, and as such was one of the hardest routes anywhere in 1983. Which of them can claim to be the first 8a in the world is moot; Tony Yaniro's 1979 *Grand Illusion*, a desperately technical overhanging corner with a thin crack at the back, is the most likely contender. *Grand Illusion* is still graded 5.13c, more like 8a+ in the French grading system. In 1983, a number of 8a routes were climbed, including several in France, not least Antoine Le Menestrel's *Rêve de Papillon* at Buoux. In Britain, the Scottish climber Dave Cuthbertson can most probably claim the prize for his 1983 climb *Requiem* at Dumbarton Rock, now regarded as 8a+, albeit one on natural protection. The rise in standards was gathering pace, not least because European climbers in particular were adapting climbing's ethical framework.

At Pen Trwyn, the gold rush of new-route development continued in 1984 much as it had the year before. The most popular crags above the Marine Drive were starting to run out of gaps so it wasn't long before climbers began exploring the steeper crag below it. Soon dubbed Lower Pen Trwyn, this is now one of the finest sport-climbing crags in Britain, albeit with the added complication that it's tidal. Andy Pollitt and Steve Lewis climbed a couple of new routes at its right-hand end in mid June, so Ben's attention was inevitably drawn to its possibilities. 'I remember looking over the wall from the Marine Drive and seeing that huge bomb bay. Hopping over the boulders at the bottom, I thought the main section would be impossible. It's so steep. But there seemed a bit of a line up the side of it.'

This main section really is a stupendous challenge, an orange-streaked and wildly overhanging wall that now holds some of Britain's best sport climbs, but in 1984 it seemed hopelessly futuristic. Ben's line climbed up relatively easily to a traverse through a large roof, which he overcame hanging first off his right heel, then his left. The wall above isn't quite so steep, but is still overhanging, and the route takes a generous crack under a flake before a final crux on a finely positioned wall. 'When I saw that line, I thought this looks really good. I started thinking: I could get a Friend in here and a nut in there. I remember looking at the start up to the traverse. It was on big holds, only about 5c, and you could have done that with nuts. But to be honest, I never really considered doing it like that. Once I'd placed one bolt, I placed another. I put in five altogether, then I started trying it and decided I needed one more. I felt the bolts would make it a better experience.'

Placing bolts on British rock had up until the 1980s been more or less forbidden, with one clear exception: aid climbing. Pen Trwyn, like several major limestone crags in Yorkshire and Derbyshire, had been a popular venue for aid climbers in the 1950s and 1960s, with some of the aid routes requiring bolts to cover gaps between pegs or nuts. (There were bolts on other types of rock, even on quarried gritstone, but these were anomalies and generally frowned upon.) During the 1970s, when rock-climbing standards began to rise quickly, many of those aid climbs were done free of their aid, but using the existing bolts as protection. On Pen Trwyn, free climbers had replaced some of these aid bolts, since salt in the sea air might have corroded them to the point they couldn't hold a fall. It didn't seem such a huge leap to put in new bolts as well.

'I didn't really think that much about it,' Ben says. 'It didn't seem like a big deal to me. None of the people I climbed with were saying to me: "You shouldn't be doing that." Even the reporting in the magazines didn't make that big a deal of it, not at the time, anyway. They did exaggerate the number of bolts I'd put in and called it Ben Moon's bolted extravaganza or something like that. But there were other routes at Pen Trwyn with six bolts. It wasn't that controversial.'

If Ben's actions didn't cause a stir among the other climbers active at Pen Trwyn that summer, his new route was seen by some as a small bomb going off deep in the foundations of British climbing, an explosion that caused this rather haphazard and gimcrack edifice to shift alarmingly. In his own engaging climbing memoir, *A Canvas of Rock*, Yorkshire climber Mark Radtke recalls stopping at Pete Livesey's cafe at Malham that summer, where climbing's brilliant, maverick modern-climbing pioneer was making his living while becoming an equally brilliant fell-runner.

'Have you heard about that young kid down in Wales?' Livesey asked Rad. 'I believe he's just done a new route at Pen Trwyn. I heard he put ten bolts in seventy feet of limestone. What do you make of that?'

Rad, still a bit hazy about exactly what Ben had done, thought ten bolts in seventy feet did sound excessive. Then again, the route was, at E7, said to be desperate. 'Well, personally,' Livesey replied, 'I can't see how a seventy-foot climb with ten bolts in it can be graded E7.'

Ben's first foray on to *Statement of Youth*. **Photo**: Phil Kelly.

Of course, Livesey was right. The grade was inappropriate since in the minds of many climbers the E7 tag carried with it some notion of risk, and how could a route with even six bolts in seventy feet be considered dangerous? That's essentially why it's now given the sport-climbing grade of French 8a. But reaching the point where British routes could be given French grades was unsurprisingly protracted and at times an agonised process. When Jerry Moffatt climbed *Revelations* that summer he told *High* magazine that he thought the grade was French 8a. 'Whatever that means,' the magazine concluded.

Ben judged his route E7 6b, but that grade took little account of the five days it took him to work out and practise the moves and then lead them without falling – what was now dubbed the redpoint. In this case, the 'E' stood for effort. 'I actually quite like that system,' Ben says, 'because it lets you give an indication of both the effort and the technical difficulty.' Most sport climbers continued to use the British system for years to come; among the first recorded uses of French grades in the new climbs book held at Stoney cafe was a route called *In Brine*, put up by Moon's friend and fellow Kingston exile Steve Lewis – in 1987.

The other startling thing about Ben's creation was the name: *Statement of Youth*. As Mark Radtke put it: 'The name appeared to have a powerful underlying message. It wasn't just a throwaway name. It appeared to be deliberately conceived, very much like the route which it described. To me, it suggested that Moon was sticking two fingers up at the old guard and saying: "Here I am, I'm here to stay and this is what the future looks like."'

That was the assumption by quite a few of the old guard too, but the name *Statement of Youth* wasn't Ben's at all. It was the inspired choice of the man holding his rope. Mark Pretty is one of Ben's most consistent training and climbing partners and had been climbing for almost ten years by the time Ben did *Statement*. In the late 1980s Mark became a sort of lightning conductor for the high-voltage outrage felt by those in the climbing establishment who feared the new European approach would undermine everything good about the British tradition. (Known universally as Zippy, his nickname isn't a nod to the garrulous puppet from the children's television show *Rainbow*, but a far more cultured reference to a character from Tod Browning's controversial 1932 film *Freaks*, which at least shows Zippy has a sense of humour.) Mark would take arguments about the ethical future of climbing head on, pointing out some of the hypocrisies of traditional climbing and on a couple of occasions placing bolts in existing free routes, which drew further ire on his head.

'It was genius, the name,' Ben says. 'It was a pun on Vera Brittain's memoir *Testament of Youth*.' Several of the landmark bolted climbs from this pivotal era had similarly futuristic names: Jerry Moffatt's *Revelations* at Raven Tor and Ron Fawcett's *New Dawn* at Malham, both climbed that summer. But *Statement of Youth*, completed by a whey-faced Londoner living in a cave, was a real challenge for those who had decided what climbing should be, even if the youth himself wasn't looking to be provocative.

'I'm not someone who seeks controversy,' Ben says. 'Having just been to France and having seen where the sport there was going, it was obvious. But I've got a mixed background with climbing. I've got one foot in the past and one in the future. I was very aware of history. I was brought up on it. But when I came into the sport, what was happening in France had a big impact on me.'

The surge in standards in the 1970s led by Tom Proctor, Pete Livesey and Ron Fawcett was, it turned out, only really the start. But the rise in technical standards couldn't continue on bold, traditional climbs, and for some rock climbers the difficulty of what they were climbing was more interesting than taking risks and exploring the psychological pressures that entailed.

'Difficulty suited me,' Ben says, which is – put simply – the kernel of his 'statement', in the same way that his father's abstract paintings were a challenge to more traditional ideas of what art should be. 'I had done quite a lot of trad climbing and if I'd wanted to continue with that, I could have done so. Trad is about controlling fear. But I was into difficulty and pure difficulty at that. Sport climbing and bouldering are about those things. The technical difficulty of trad climbs is a million miles away from what's done on the hardest sport routes.'

The accusation Ben and his sport-climbing contemporaries faced was that this new development would undermine the traditional values of the sport. Suddenly, rock climbing was no longer about some intense, exploratory psychological narrative but a dry mathematical formula involving training and power-to-weight ratios. One of the old guard dubbed the new generation as 'anorexic young weirdos', whose obsession – itself the name of a famous sport climb at Malham – with numbers was driving the richness and depth out of climbing.

Jim Perrin, writing in *Climber* magazine, wondered about the intensity and focus of sport climbing, and how it failed to connect with the majority of climbers operating in a more traditional context. 'I'd love to hear more refined accounts and representations of the objective detail, which resonates out to within reach of the imaginative grasp of common experience.' Or to put it more simply: What does this offer the rest of us? Where are the stories? 'But perhaps at the end,' Perrin concluded, 'the performer only exists in the absorption within his art, perhaps is reaching the incommunicable.'

In an editorial in *High* magazine titled *British Climbing Rest in Peace*, Geoff Birtles, describing British climbing as a 'very rare and beautiful flower', mourned its passing: 'Ask yourself, what does climbing become if the elements of danger and uncertainty are removed, which is precisely what has happened to the vast majority of new climbs pioneered in Britain today. I suggest the answer is that it is no longer rock climbing but quite another beast tamed to suit the trainer and about as fearsome as a bull with no balls … The notion of ethics, as we quaintly called our unwritten rules, is also gone, leaving an ungoverned shambles.'

The unwritten rules of climbing were often evoked in this period. Geoff Milburn, who oversaw guidebooks produced by the British

Mountaineering Council and the Climbers' Club, wrote an opinion piece in *High* magazine extolling the freedom of the hills, before setting out a detailed nineteen-point code of conduct for climbers to follow. 'Climbers without a deep feel for the way that the British climbing ethic has evolved place bolts indiscriminately either to remove the death potential or to reduce the standard of the route to their own level.'

This wave of opposition to sport climbing, some of it coherent, much of it not, and the sense that a noble tradition was about to expire, was hopelessly overstated. The mid 1980s not only saw the arrival of sport climbing in Britain, they also proved to be one of the golden ages of traditional climbing. Even as sport climbing took off, there was a new wave of exploration on the sea cliffs at Gogarth that saw some of its boldest and best routes added. For every Ben Moon there was a Johnny Dawes or Nick Dixon. Those concerned about the impact of sport climbing will argue that their intervention helped preserve the old against the new, especially when the British experience is contrasted with what happened in Europe, where many existing routes had bolts added and holds were routinely chipped. Yet there was never any real danger that a century of tradition was about to be wiped out.

'One of the great things about British climbing,' Ben says, 'is that you can do whatever you like. We've got some of the best trad in the world. We've also got some good sport climbing and bouldering. Ken Wilson was very anti the whole sport-climbing thing and some of the things he came out with were rubbish. I remember him saying he didn't understand sport climbing. That if you spend enough time practising the route then you'd inevitably do it. But that's obviously not the case. Ken's fears that there would be bolts up *Right Wall* on Dinas Cromlech didn't materialise. I do have reservations about retro-bolting that's happened on limestone, but that's about all.'

He may not have sought controversy but Ben wasn't averse to stating his mind when he saw something he didn't like. In 1986, at Rubicon Wall in the Derbyshire dale of Water-cum-Jolly, he had a spat with another leading sport climber of the day, Chris Gore, who snatched a project Ben had been trying from under his nose and added a bolt. (Ben later extended this route, dubbed *Kudos*, by a few feet to give a more substantial problem and called it *Hot Fun Closing*.)

Infuriated by this gamesmanship and what he felt to be an inappropriate use of a drill, Ben weighed in, writing in the new-routes book held at Stoney cafe that he protested 'strongly against the bolt that has been placed but it seems that if I were to remove it, it will cause even more aggression between certain people than there is at the moment. I realise that there has been a misunderstanding but maybe we should all just think a little bit more before it's all too late. The bolt will remain.'

For his part, Chris Gore, Ben recalls, suggested Ben was becoming a bit of a brat and compared him to Jerry Moffatt. A more laconic perspective came from Christian Griffith, the brilliant American sport climber and founder of apparel company Verve. In a letter to Ben he wrote: 'How's this route *Hot Fun Closing*? Sounds mega-hard. But, really man, Rubicon? Couldn't you have picked a better spot for one of Britain's hardest routes?'

The new routes books at Stoney, now helpfully digitised by Phil Kelly and available online, offer a blow-by-blow and often quite funny real-time record of British climbing's growing pains.[1] So many angels, so many pins. In the mid 1980s, the amount of abusive marginalia increased sharply as passions ran hot – along with the occasional nugget of useful wisdom. Although friends, Ben disagreed with Mark Pretty about the addition of extra bolts to a Ron Fawcett route, *Tequila Mockingbird*, at Chee Tor – and said so publicly in the Stoney book: 'A substantial proportion of Peak District climbers after much deliberation feels that five bolts are excessive. If you must do it, replace the two bolts but anything else would change the character of the route.'

1 www.philkelly.com/rockarchivist

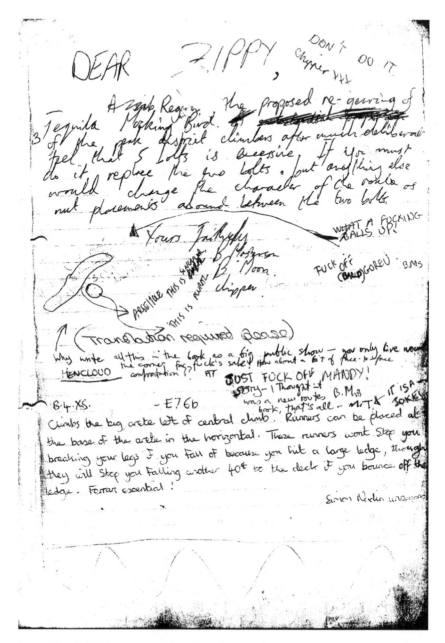

An extract from the 1986 Stoney new routes book. **Photo:** Courtesy of Phil Kelly/Rock Archivist.

Ben and two friends, Ben Masterson and Keith Jones, signed this statement, prompting some wag to cross out the words 'substantial proportion' and write 'three' instead. Someone else scrawled: 'Why write this in the book as a public show – you only live five minutes round the corner for fuck's sake. How about a bit of face to face?' These are, as an aside, the sort of comments you now get on an internet forum. Most climbers roll their eyes and move on when they come across this kind of exchange, but to those involved the debate can seem incredibly intense. Mark Pretty was cast as the villain, which he cheerfully acknowledged at Pen Trwyn in the name of one of his best and most popular new routes – *I've Been a Bad, Bad Boy*.

For those who think internet trolling marks a new low in human behaviour, the new routes book at Stoney could be as direct and nasty as any Twitter-storm. Take this advice, directed personally to Ben, about gardening: 'Any new routes being put up with extreme gardening, such as using a jack to lever a huge ledge off a crag will, once climbed, be abseiled down and the holds removed with a little hammer. This sort of gardening by you so-called rock stars will fuck up climbing for good in the Peak, so be warned. Dare try it in Yorkshire and your balls will go missing (if you have any).' Testicles featured a lot in the abuse of sport climbers in this era.

Climbing has always had its heroes and villains, even before the advent of magazines and websites, but the arrival of climbing media distorted and magnified this process, sometimes unfairly. Ben was now part of this process. As a schoolboy at Christ's Hospital he had pored over climbing magazines, soaking up the culture and cast list of his passion as though what he read was the absolute truth. After climbing *Statement of Youth*, he found himself included. 'I'll always remember seeing my photo in the magazines for the first time, a little photo that Geoff Birtles took of me standing under *Oedipus* at Froggatt Edge with a toothbrush between my teeth.'

1 *Hoop-La*, acrylic on canvas, July 1965. Jeremy Moon (1934–1973). © Estate of Jeremy Moon.
Photo: © Tate, London 2015.

2 Jeremy Moon outside his flat/studio on Chepstow Road, London in 1963. **Photo**: Moon Family Collection.
3 Beth and Jeremy, with (L–R) Georgina, Robert and Ben in 1972. **Photo**: Moon Family Collection.

CHRIST'S HOSPITAL

REPORT FOR ...SUMMER... TERM 19.82

NAME ..MOON...B.J.... HOUSE ...LAMB...B.. **GREAT ERASMUS**

AGE (at end of term) ......16.1...... AVERAGE AGE OF BLOCK (at end of term) .....16.4......

Column (a) shows the form or set with the number of forms or sets within the block, (b) the place within the form or set, and (c) the predicted O level grade. The addition of + or – to the grade indicates either above average effort or the lack of it.

	(a)	(b)		(c)
ENGLISH	M/8		The occasional good essay suggests the possibility of a pass. It will need more concentration than he normally shows.	CD
HISTORY	K/2		His documentary work has been erratic. At his best he will secure a C.	C/2
FRENCH	6/8	12/12	28%: Has made no serious effort in this subject. WL.	E/F
MATHEMATICS	6/7	12/17	Still erratic and undisciplined in his approach to work. Some of his practice papers have reached a pass level.	C/D
PHYSICS				
CHEMISTRY	8/8	8/12	A real 'touch and go' situation. Very difficult to predict since his efforts are extremely erratic.	S/D
BIOLOGY	8/8	8/12		C/D
..Drama... (option 1)		8/8	I hope to see some eleventh hour determination to catch up with coursework notes & material. He has worked well on the practical side, but has not had the same determination for the theory.	D/E
..History... (option 2)	2	2/2	Some of his practice answers have reached the required standard but he hasn't been consistent enough to feel secure.	C/D

Housemaster: HISTORY PROJECT! Difficult to assess, his work is thoughtful & interesting, but limited in range & scope.
This is not, I am afraid, a satisfactory report - particularly in his O level term. What is highlighted above is Ben's inability to commit himself to academic study; this aimlessness also extends to other areas of life too. It is, in fact, only in climbing that he finds purpose and the maturity to see that he need to strive in other areas too is still lacking. Ben's future is very unclear but I hope everything works out well for him and brings him happiness.

Headmaster: I agree: this report cannot be called satisfactory, but we all hope that he will achieve some success in the examinations, sufficient to assist him in the future. We wish him well.

4

5–6 Ben in Wales with Ric Potter, 1982.
7 Ben on pitch 1 of the *Direct Route*, Milestone Buttress. **Photos**: Ric Potter.

8 *Chimpanzodrome* at Le Saussois, France, 1984. **Photo**: Jerry Moffatt.
9 *Main Overhang* at Malham Cove, 1984. **Photo**: Ben Moon Collection.

10 1984 and the first ascent of *Statement of Youth*, Lower Pen Trwyn, Wales. **Photo**: Steve Lewis.
11 Bouldering at Klagemauer, Germany, in 1985. **Photo**: Jerry Moffatt.
12 Buoux, 1985: the crux move of *Chouca*. **Photo**: Steve Lewis.

13 & 14 Buoux, 1986: *La Rose et le Vampire*, Buoux. **Photos**: Ben Moon Collection.
15 *Zeke the Freak*, Rubicon Wall, Derbyshire. **Photo**: Richie Brooks.

16 & 17 Buoux, 1988: *Le Minimum*. **Photos**: Ben Moon Collection/Steve Lewis.
18 *La Mission*, Buoux. **Photo**: Richie Brooks.

19–20 *Agincourt*. **Photos:** Takashi Nakagawa.

21 *West Side Story*, Burbage.
22 Blindfolded dynos at Stoney Middleton. **Photos**: Jerry Moffatt.

23 Steve Lewis, Mark 'Zippy' Pretty and Ben at Raven Tor, 1991. **Photo**: Richie Brooks.
24 Jerry Moffatt and Ben. **Photo**: Steve Lewis.

25 *Hubble*. **Photo:** Steve Lewis.

This postage-stamp of an image, murky and grey, marked some sort of approbation from the scruffy and quarrelsome community he now lived in. When Steve Board, an old school friend, wrote to him asking for advice about what sort of rucksack he should buy Ben replied thoughtfully and usefully, and then mentioned the route: 'If you buy the September issue of *High* and go to near the back there's a small portrait of me. What do you reckon to it? It may seem really insignificant to you, I don't know, but it's really good seeing your photo in a magazine like that for the first time.'

Like most people who find what they do being reported by the media, Ben soon discovered the process can be unbalanced and inaccurate, that editors have their favourites, and are not always as conscientious as you might expect in finding out what the story is, rather than merely accepting what they're given. Often they stick to their own prejudices. Unlike Jerry, Ben wasn't adept at building a public persona that would give him leverage with potential sponsors – nor was he particularly interested. 'Jerry liked being well known, but I didn't, not really. I wasn't climbing to be well known.' It would take a while before he made the connection between using his name and earning a living.

Jerry's climbing career had begun in a context that was both comfortable and comprehensible to climbers who had been at their peak in the 1960s and 1970s. His new climb *Master's Wall* at Cloggy and his solo ascents of famous Dinas Cromlech routes like *Right Wall* were greeted with amazed applause. The new cohort that followed close behind him bringing new ideas and conflicting ethics was much more alarming. Jerry had been embraced as the next new thing; Ben was not. He'd sent his first new route to Pete Livesey, a scruffy, loose E1 that was quickly forgotten, just two years before. Now, after only a few months of serious effort, he had not only climbed one of the hardest and best new routes in the world, he had used a new kind of paradigm that offered huge potential to push technical standards.

A young, photogenic climber on the cusp of the latest developments espousing a new ethical framework would, you might think, make for a story. But it would be five years before anyone in the British climbing community published an interview with Ben – and *Statement of Youth* was omitted altogether from the landmark book *Extreme Rock*, co-authored by Ken Wilson and Bernard Newman. (Interviews in the European press were more frequent.) The lack of information about Ben, and his relative indifference to pushing himself into the limelight, made him an enigmatic if striking figure in British climbing, certainly in the 1980s. When his friend Sean Myles interviewed him first, after the first ascents of *Agincourt* and *Maginot Line*, he asked him directly about his lack of exposure. 'It would be nice to be appreciated,' Ben said, 'but that only matters if people actually understand what you're doing. The British press is not very enthusiastic.'

If the older generation failed to appreciate or understand what Ben had done, his contemporaries did not. 'Straight away, everybody wanted to do the route. It really wasn't that controversial with those around me and the proof was in *Statement's* popularity. Younger climbers understood where things were going.'

It might have proved appealing, but it took some time for most of the leading British climbers of that era to repeat *Statement*. Jerry, on the other hand, was there almost immediately. He took Ben's suggestion that the route might take him a few days as a personal challenge and fired the thing off in a day – just.

'Did that hurt?'

'Not really,' Ben says. 'I didn't have any pretensions about where I was at. Jerry was still quite a bit better than me in the summer of 1984.'

At least Jerry found the route 'harder than I was expecting', and admired its quality. Today *Statement* is acknowledged as among the very best of its grade anywhere in Britain and an unavoidable milestone for aspiring sport climbers attempting the magical eighth grade. As Jerry wrote in his memoirs: 'Ultimately, what won through was the quality of the route.'

Ben's own personal reaction was curiously muted. 'I remember doing the heel-hook traverse and thinking it was pretty cool, but I don't remember how I felt when I did it. I didn't think I'd done anything exceptional.' Ben had turned eighteen a couple of weeks before climbing *Statement* and was still on a wildly steep trajectory of improvement. 'I didn't really understand what I had done or where I was at. After *Hubble* or *Agincourt*, yes. But when I did *Statement* I hadn't really done that many hard routes. The hardest had been 7c+ in France and trying *Fissure Serge* at 7c+. I'd come back and done *Strawberries* and *Tequila Mockingbird*, but that was about it.'

As news of *Statement* and its implications began to sink in, Ben's position in the climbing world would begin to change. But that summer he was still much the scruffy urchin that had slept rough at Fontainebleau the winter before – although turning eighteen did increase his dole by an extra ten pounds a week. For life's little luxuries, like batteries for a cassette player, there was always shoplifting, a widespread and long-established habit in the climbing community whatever your ethical stance on the placement of bolts.

Pocketing his free batteries in Llandudno Woolworths, Ben attracted the attention of the security guard, dressed in suit and tie and black leather shoes. 'He chased us for about half an hour. The guy was incredible. He chased us all the way up to the Grand Hotel and then down the pier. We hid on the beach behind a shed but when we stuck our heads round to take a peek he was powering towards us across the sand. Eventually we lost him at the train station.'

Then, as teenage boys are prone to do, they completely forgot about their close call and went to eat at the National Milk Bar, now closed but once part of a chain that covered much of Wales and the West Midlands. The Llandudno branch opened in 1934 – just down the road from Woolworths. Pretty soon the police turned up and arrested Ben and his partner in crime and took them to the station.

'You did, at the time, have quite a distinctive barnet?'

'Yeah. Stupid, eh? Being the only person in Llandudno with dreads, hanging out just down the road from the scene of the crime.'

A few days shy of his eighteenth birthday, the police promised him that if he confessed the crime, he'd walk free. 'So I thought, great, I want to get out of here and admitted to it.' The name *Statement of Youth* had other connotations. 'They immediately charged me and I spent the night in the cells. Maybe that's where my distrust of the police comes from. I was up before the magistrate next day and let off with a caution. The one good thing was they served me eggs for breakfast in the morning.'

Ben was far from being alone in such delinquent behaviour. On the evening of the day he climbed *Statement of Youth*, the police arrived at the National Milk Bar mob-handed with three squad cars and made eight arrests. It's fair to say that some of the 'tricks' climbers had developed to survive on benefits and go climbing were exhausting the patience of local businesses. As Chris Gore put it: 'The nights of free baths in hotels and hours spent in cafes with only one cup of tea are over.' All the climbers were released without charge.

Like a nomadic – and skint – tribe, Britain's sport climbers decamped from Pen Trwyn that summer and moved on to Malham Cove in Yorkshire. Ben went there first on a day of heavy rain, stopping at Pete Livesey's cafe in the village, where the proprietor, that gnomic, teasing master of Yorkshire limestone, served his dreadlocked customer tea and kept his counsel. What had brought Ben and his friends from Sheffield was the promise of fresh hunting grounds for new routes to be climbed in the French style. Like Pen Trwyn, Malham had been popular with aid climbers, so there were plenty of objectives to climb free, and blank acres of rock in between that would only be done free with bolts.

In 1984, the intense interest in Malham among sport climbers was only just starting to build. That summer Rob Gawthorpe climbed the first pitch of a 1960s aid route, *Main Overhang*. Ron Fawcett added what is still one of the best sport routes of its grade, *New Dawn*. Scanning the centre of this vast amphitheatre, Ben could see only a handful of free routes, but at his back heard the ominous sound of an approaching stampede. He started on *Main Overhang*:

'As soon as I started I knew that the climbing was going to suit me. I realised a lot of the difficulty was going to be in finding the holds quickly enough, because the rock was striped in black and white, which seemed to hide the finger-holds. Below and across the other side of the cove Martin Atkinson was working on *New Dawn*. The climbing on this was totally different from *Main Overhang*. It overhung considerably and required powerful climbing on big holds. Not my scene at all.'

Ben almost managed to repeat *Main Overhang* that day, but as the light failed a stroke of bad luck foiled his efforts. 'I felt good, relaxed, psyched, and the pain in my fingers was no longer there, I'd shut it out. I couldn't believe it – all those moves I had found so hard felt so easy, even the hard crux moves I had been falling off passed by with only the slightest hesitation, I had the final layaway in my hand, one move, just one move, my heart was going like nothing else. Walking my feet up the rock and pulling in to reach for the jugs the layaway snapped.'

He was back the next day, and the route soon succumbed. Now he looked for something new to try. 'There were two main aid lines up the centre of Malham Cove, the *Directissima* and the *Superdirectissima*. It was the top pitches I was interested in, because the lower pitches looked too hard. But I was slow off the mark and Martin, on his rest day, had nipped in and already cleaned the *Directissima*'s top pitch. I wasn't bothered because I felt the *Superdirectissima* was the better line.'

Ben focused on the route's second pitch, right at the centre of the cove and accessed from a terrace halfway up the crag that petered out at the start of the pitch. Although not steep – for the most part the route was just off vertical with an overhanging start – it was nevertheless technically difficult and Ben took an hour to figure out a sequence through the crux, by which stage he was exhausted so he stopped for lunch. That afternoon he came close to finishing the route, and was confident of success next morning:

'Quickly running the moves through my mind, I set off up the slightly leaning wall. The moves felt hard but I was going well. Suddenly disaster struck. Halfway through the last difficult moves, twenty feet from the belay and looking at a monster fall, I awoke from my concentration. I had forgotten to clip any of the bolts. I quickly got to grips with the situation, clipped into the nearest bolts and lowered down to the stance to gather myself. I couldn't believe it. Neither could anyone else, for that matter. They were all laughing at me.'

With the sequence wired, success was only briefly postponed, but the route's position high above the ground and powerfully exposed began to prey on his mind. 'Although the route is only seventy feet long, the terrific exposure makes it feel twice that. Nearing the top I moved right to a line of big flakes, where I started to get gripped, thinking I was going to fall off but I moved up and made a few tricky moves to the ledge.' A pitch that began halfway up the crag and finished some way short of its top was complete, a foreign notion to many climbers, but not to a group of people who were now thinking more about sequences of moves and less about their context. He called it *Free 'n' Easy* and graded it E6 6c, the same grade as *Main Overhang* and *New Dawn*. All three routes, like almost every other hard route at Malham, are now given French grades; *Free 'n' Easy* is rated 7c and has been absorbed into longer routes, climbed as standards have risen.

In retrospect, Malham, one of England's grandest views, was the ideal arena for rock climbing's newest incarnation. It offered a sweeping stage for an era of performance; the white rock proved the perfect backdrop for the colourful Lycra tights and ripped torsos of its new adherents. Ben, along with Andy Pollitt, was one of the few men who could get away with Lycra. Within a couple of years, this white canvas would, from a distance, seem dotted with colourful blobs, like an abstract painting. As you approached, the blobs would assume the honed shapes of climbers resting, hanging on the rope, trying a move or slumping back on to the gear, their seconds' eyes often glazed with boredom. Most were congregated along what was soon dubbed the Catwalk, a broad ledge running across the base of the crag. There would be a lot of banter and the atmosphere was very male, and very competitive. Dossing out on Windy Ledge, wearing fibre pile and taking the piss out of anyone who got ahead of himself – that world was gone, just as Mrs Thatcher overturned the post-war consensus and hammered the unions.

Many climbers took on the new ethic of practice and redpoint, and added a couple of grades overnight. It didn't necessarily make them better climbers, but the air of self-congratulation was tangible at Malham. Gill Kent memorably described the crag's faithful as 'peacocks in a concrete zoo'. Mark Radtke wondered whether concentrating on measurement and performance was limiting the sport: 'It seemed that now, the number alone was becoming the holy grail of rock climbing and those in search of it were at risk of losing touch with the element that, in my opinion, actually breathes 'soul' into a rather irrational pursuit.'

Grades have always motivated climbers, to a lesser or greater extent, in whatever form the game is practised: sport, trad or 8,000-metre peaks. But in the 1980s things changed. An exponential rise in the quality of colour printing and the bright colours and chiselled bodies of sport climbing combined to immense effect right across Europe – if not immediately in Britain. Big numbers became an easy headline and a result for sponsors and sponsored climbers alike. The buzz, and the excitement of this new, safer form of climbing, was palpable. It would not only transform the ethics of the sport, its easy appeal attracted thousands of new young climbers and with them more money. The challenge for Ben Moon and the other climbers leading this revolution was to test the limits of what a human body could achieve when fear was no longer part of the equation. For Ben, it would be a long journey.

Chouca, Buoux, 1985. **Photo:** Ben Moon Collection.

ZEKE THE
FREAK

Given that in a year Ben had gone from being unknown to being recognised as among the very best handful of climbers in Britain, the suggestion that he spent the next couple of years drifting a little might seem surprising, even ridiculous, especially when you consider what he managed in that period, roughly the summer of 1985 to 1987. His exploits in Britain and France earned him an invitation to the embryonic competition circuit where he had some early successes, and he continued to repeat some of the hardest routes being done by his peers and to add significant new ones of his own. And yet: 'It's funny you ask me what I was doing in that period,' Ben says, 'because, to be honest, I wasn't doing a great deal. It was a bit of a waste of a couple of years.'

Having closed the gulf between himself and other leading British climbers, the rise in technical standards in Europe in the mid 1980s left all of them, Ben included, a little behind – and the fact that this was happening was revealed in the most dramatic way imaginable.

In the summer of 1985, Jibé Tribout and twenty-year-old Antoine Le Menestrel came to Britain to try the hard new sport routes being done by Jerry Moffatt and the pack of mostly Sheffield-based climbers pushing back the boundaries. (An exception was Manchester climber Tony Ryan, whose 1986 route *Caviar* at Rubicon was another contender for the first 8a+ in the Peak District.) The French dossed in Sheffield on Martin

Atkinson's floor at Hunter House Road – 84, not 124, an altogether more serious address, packed to the rafters with sport-climbing beef – and, thanks to the wet weather that July, spent a lot of time under the shelter of Raven Tor, repeating Jerry's *Revelations*, arguably the first 8a+ in Britain. (Having suffered broken holds, it is now often regarded as 8b.) Ben also repeated the route, but that same afternoon Antoine did something that left British climbing's collective jaw on the floor.

He soloed it.

Given that a fall from the route's defining feature, an impossibly smooth groove that had once looked all but unclimbable, would have left Antoine with at best a broken back, it was a shocking achievement. The photograph of him perched at the start of this sequence high above the ground is still impressive, even after three decades. Chris Gore was right at the heart of the intensely competitive climbing scene in Sheffield at that time and understood exactly what had just happened. He wrote in *High* magazine: 'For a long time now we have nestled in our own cocoon of complacency, believing that British is always best and paying no heed to the doings of foreign climbers; such are the foibles of a myopic society.'

For Ben, Antoine's effort was also sobering.

'They absolutely creamed it. I was shocked. I'd still be impressed if someone came up and soloed it today.'

'Did it make you think that you weren't in the ball park?'

'Yes, probably, a little bit. I thought I was good but I thought Antoine was a better climber and that I had a way to go.'

'Did you want to be as good as him? Was that your ambition?'

'I'd like to think that I didn't just want to be the best climber in the world. I think I wanted to be the best climber I possibly could. If that meant I became one of the best, then that was good. But it was never a goal. I've always had that attitude.'

As you might expect, Jerry's reaction to Le Menestrel's feat was cooler, but his more grudging admiration shows the scale of what had been done:

'I knew it was possible. I wasn't that impressed because I'd climbed with Antoine the winter before in Joshua Tree and had been climbing better than him. But in retrospect it was a very, very impressive ascent.'

It hadn't been Antoine's intention to belittle what Jerry Moffatt had achieved. He had previous experience of British climbing, making an ascent of *Right Wall* at the age of fifteen, a seminal experience in his development as a climber. And even if he didn't already admire British climbing, it wasn't part of Antoine's repertoire to make statements like that. 'No one kicks anyone's ass, that's not the point,' Marc Le Menestrel said years later, after making a fast repeat of the Stanage boulder problem *Brad Pit*. 'And I do not think that Antoine felt like this when he did *Revelations*. I haven't kicked anyone's ass – on the contrary. For me coming here helps me to be modest, to learn things.'

On this occasion it worked the other way round. There was a great deal to be learned from the Parisians quickly slicing their way through some of Britain's hardest routes. Because not only did Antoine solo *Revelations*, he and Jibé made some impressive ascents of other hard climbs at Raven Tor. Chris Gore wasn't the only one to wonder what their routes were like, given what short work they'd made of ours. 'There are approximately twenty routes of 8a, ten of which are as hard as *Revelations* and five that are certainly harder.' Christian Griffith, not only a participant but also a great observer of these revolutionary times, put it succinctly: 'There was this international rivalry. We were all going on the heels of Jerry Moffatt at one time. Bachar was first, then Jerry took over, then the French, then Wolfgang built his Campus board and started training his ass off and did all these brutal routes.'

Antoine's solo ascent of *Revelations* marked the moment when the French ascendancy became clear to the British climbing public, although top British climbers heading out to Germany and France, as Ben had done, were more aware of what was happening on the Continent. The October before, Wolfgang Güllich had made the first ascent of what is generally recognised as the first 8b – *Kanal im Rücken*, and in April 1985 climbed *Punks in the Gym* at Australia's Arapiles, the likeliest contender for the first 8b+. Antoine's younger brother Marc did the second 8b in 1985 at Buoux, *Les Mains Sales*. (Or 'Dirty Hands' – a play by Jean-Paul Sartre. Contrast this with the fondness among some British climbers for names involving Arnold Schwarzenegger.) By 1986 there was a steely-fingered clutch of 8b+s, including Antoine's *La Rage de Vivre* and Jibé's *To Bolt or Not to Be* at Smith Rock in the US, the route that made it plain that America's free-climbing dominance was well and truly over.

Since the early 1980s, Jerry Moffatt had been the most dynamic force in British climbing, someone eager to test himself with the hardest routes abroad and against the best climbers in the world. In late 1984 he had left for another trip to the States, climbing the classic Yosemite 5.13a crack *The Phoenix* on sight, which, like Le Menestrel's effort at Raven Tor, left the locals scratching their heads a little. But Moffatt's body, after years of intense training, particularly on Bachar ladders, was starting to break down.

In the course of a long letter, Christian Griffith told Ben in the spring of 1985 about his encounter with a stricken Moffatt: 'Heard from Jerry lately? I got back from Joshua Tree a few weeks ago. Jerry was there but he said he was way fucked up – tendonitis in both elbows and one shoulder. He may also have capsulitis, which is a wearing down of the covering protecting the bones of the joint. He said he hadn't climbed in a few months but hoped to be well in one or two more. Bachar was paying for his physiotherapy so he will probably recover fast and strong and financially secure. I asked him how his trip to the Valley was. He said he flashed *Phoenix*! Unfortunately, he said he probably wouldn't come to Colorado as he says he would be way too 'twisted' seeing all of the routes and not being able to climb. As for me, expect to see me this summer in England probably around July to August after I go to the Valley and Smith Rocks. Write me man, I want to know what's been going on.'

What had been going on was an acceleration of standards brought on by a sharper focus and better training. Christian had, as he often did, teased Ben in his letter about the scruffy crags British climbers eulogised. 'Training British-style is definitely the ticket but American potential is way better. So come here and climb.' Only, as it soon became clear, training British-style wasn't quite the ticket after all. Nor were British sport-climbing ethics yet quite analogous with the equivalent French version. Ben had used a form of yo-yoing on his ascent of *Revelations* and hadn't yet mastered the subtleties of climbing by redpointing in the way that Antoine and Jibé had. This was one of the things that would cost him in this period.

As an example, in the autumn of 1986 he came very close to making the second ascent of *La Rage de Vivre*, which was among the hardest routes in the world at that stage. 'I very nearly did *Rage*, but I wasn't very professional about it. I was redpointing, but didn't work the top section enough. I fell off it five or six times and shouldn't have. I had done Marc's other hard routes, like *Chouca* and *La Rose et le Vampire*. I knew I could do it.'

Tactical naiveté wasn't the only problem. The pace of change in rock climbing during the 1980s was quite staggering, with grades climbing essentially from 8a to 9a in less than a decade. In the 1980s, a year could make 'a very, very big difference' as Jerry Moffatt observed. In April 1987, just months after the first 8b+ appeared, Wolfgang Güllich climbed *Wall Street* on the Krottenseer Turm in a remote corner of the Frankenjura, a sequence of fierce pulls on limestone finger pockets that required a brutal amount of power. (A hold on the route was improved afterwards, prompting Güllich, one of the ethical heroes of this period, to fill the pocket in completely with cement. The new version of the route is often considered to be the first 8c in the world.)

Wolfgang was a naturally powerful climber, his biographer Tilmann Hepp speculating that there never was a climber 'with so much maximal strength. There were others who approached it, like the Englishman

Ben Moon, but when Güllich was in shape hardly anyone came close.' So why didn't Ben make as much progress as Wolfgang in these years?

One answer lurked near Wolfgang's house in Oberschöllenbach. He had put together a training facility in his cellar at home, but had grown increasingly bored with it. Climbers had been training their stamina for years, but Wolfgang wanted to find a method to train his power, that explosive short-term effort, and so climb harder moves. He drew on theory and practice developed by Soviet athletics coaches and dubbed in America 'plyometrics'. Although the term is a bit misleading, the regime focuses on extending and then abruptly contracting muscles in order to train specifically to maximise their power. Wolfgang came up with an overhanging board with finger edges of various depths set at regular intervals that he could climb up using just his fingers – no feet. Lacking the necessary space, he installed the board in a corner of his local gym, the Campus Centre. Now there are Campus boards at climbing walls around the world. (You can track the arrival of training for power in Britain by new route names, not least Ben's own route, *Pump up the Power*, an 8a+ done in this period at Raven Tor.) Ben would become a master at this form of training, devising training methods and programmes on it that are still in use today.

Along with Güllich's innovation, there is now also a small library of training advice and a legion of experts writing blogs with competing ideas on how best to train for rock climbing. In the 1980s, climbers were making it up as they went along, with not much to draw on, learning from each other and making similar mistakes. Jerry's long break from climbing was the direct consequence of over-training; he rarely had a rest day, climbing all the time and when it was raining doing pull-ups. 'I was sleeping in barns and caves where it's damp, not warming up properly, surviving on a poor diet. It builds up and you pay for it some day.'

Moffatt's injury, coinciding with Antoine Le Menestrel's solo ascent of *Revelations*, took some of the impetus out of British climbing. Ron Fawcett,

Ben on The School Room Campus board. **Photo:** Steve Lewis.

Ben's idol, was also increasingly absent, finding himself out of kilter with the modern era of training and redpointing, even though in 1985 he climbed his own 8a – the much-admired *Zoolook* at Malham. 'Having done my fair share of hard routes on limestone over the years,' he said, 'I could see that things were only going to get tougher and that meant just one thing – more training.'

Having sprinted through the grades to join the world's elite, Ben didn't yet have a plan on how to take things forward. At the age Ben was now, Jerry had been flying round the world repeating the hardest routes available in the best style with the stated ambition of wanting to be seen as the best. Johnny Dawes had left school at eighteen with an exercise book full of imaginative unclimbed lines he'd spotted during his apprenticeship. Ben's exceptional contribution would be to push technical standards to new limits, but realising this goal needed time – and a sharper focus. It would take a minor crisis to set him back on course.

'I think I was missing a sense of direction a little bit,' he says. 'My brother had moved to Sheffield to study art, and I was living with him and Keith Jones on Woodstock Road. I wasn't living with really keen climbers.' A letter co-written by Ben and Quentin Fisher to Jerry, going quietly crazy recuperating from his injury at Wolfgang's house in Oberschöllenbach, is a rambling, dope-fuelled update on recent events – driving lessons where handbrake turns are discouraged, a proposed trip to Manchester to drop acid, mechanical problems with Ben's bike, news of a friend sent to prison for animal rights activism – and Ben's plans to redpoint his project at Rubicon before leaving for his competition debut in Italy.[1]

Much is made of the competition between Jerry and Ben, and certainly

---

1 The trip to Manchester had a curious footnote. Hanging out in Manchester Polytechnic's students' union bar, Quentin, Helen Brown and Ben were approached by someone from the band Simply Red, asking if they'd like to appear in their next video, to be shot the following Tuesday in the now demolished 'Crescents' housing estate in Hulme, a haven for students, artistic types and addicts following Manchester City Council's decision to stop collecting rents there. In the released video for *Red Box*, Quentin and Helen are clearly spotted dancing at a student party, but Ben is strangely absent. A discarded cut of the video, briefly available online, had a sequence featuring Mick Hucknall dancing with Ben and there's no doubt who looks the cooler rock star.

in this phase of his career, Ben missed the sense of purpose Jerry always carried with him. But there was an important difference between them; Jerry thrived on having the edge over his peers, whereas Ben didn't. On more than one occasion in this period, after Jerry recovered from his surgery, he would swoop down and pick off problems Ben had been working on, like *Superman* at Crag X in Cressbrook, or *Jerry's Traverse* at Stanage. 'I think I was just better at finishing,' Jerry recalled, 'finishing something off, better under pressure. Ben [Moon] and Stuart [Cameron] were often bouldering so much better than me, but we'd try stuff and I could just sit down and rest, and then pull it out of the bag because I really wanted to do problems before everybody else.'

Although at nineteen and twenty Ben didn't have bigger priorities than climbing, he had plenty of distractions. He shared his father's love of motorsport in general and motorbikes in particular, so having spent years hitching to the crag he was more than happy when his mother offered to buy him a two-stroke Yamaha 125cc. Later she helped him buy a bigger bike, a Kawasaki GPz 550 – just saying the name prompts Ben to smile a little at the memory of it. For now, he had to content himself bombing out to Raven Tor or Water-cum-Jolly on his 125 or taking turns on Jerry's powerful Suzuki GSX-R 1100 in Germany, where Jerry was recovering from surgery on his elbows. Ben had intended to have a fortnight testing himself on routes in the Frankenjura, but instead spent them racing up and down the region's winding roads. On one sharp bend, unused to the much better brakes on Jerry's machine, Ben locked the front brake and lost control, sending them both sliding along the tarmac and the bike into a hedge, where it hung upside down, rear wheel spinning forlornly to a stop. Ben was furious with himself, tossing aside his helmet and stomping off, which Jerry found hilarious. But with his father's death an ever-present memory, the balance between excitement and caution must have been hard to regulate sometimes.

'I had an accident on the Yamaha as well,' he says a little ruefully.

Outside a pub in Sheffield, a car pulled out in front of him and Ben went over the bonnet, but neither bike nor rider was damaged. It was a curious echo of the prang his father had suffered on Chepstow Road in London, which resulted in him finding a studio. More serious was an accident Ben had the following year, in 1987. Speeding out to the crag from Sheffield past the Grouse Inn, there's an awkward right-hand bend with a layby that's popular with climbers and walkers accessing Froggatt Edge. The layby is bordered by a steep grassy slope about ten feet high, which ends at a drystone wall.

By this stage Ben had a car, a beat-up gold Volkswagen Scirocco. He failed to make the bend and shot up the bank and into the wall. The Scirocco bounced off this, sending blocks of gritstone flying, and landed back on its roof in the layby. He crawled out of the window and walked down the hill to a garage to get the Scirocco towed, before hitching back to Sheffield. The return of the Scirocco, arriving in Sheffield on the back of the tow-truck, crushed and broken, alarmed Quentin Fisher who saw it driven past him on the street.

The accident's aftermath included a letter from the Peak Park Planning Board: 'Dear Mr Moor [sic], I understand that a gold Scirocco in your ownership was recently involved in an accident in which approximately six metres of wall on the Board's Eastern Moors was demolished. As this authority has no impact insurance, I must recover the cost of the repair, which will be £12 per metre plus VAT.'

Even that wasn't Ben's closest call, which came instead driving back to Buoux a couple of years later, after climbing *Maginot Line* at Volx. Johnny was driving this time, in his Peugeot 205 1.9 GTI. Jerry Moffatt and Chris Plant were in the back seat: 'It was dark, and everyone was buzzing. We were on the road just before Céreste, which is brilliant fun. There are two right-handers that are quite similar, only one is tighter than the other and he got the bends mixed up and went into the tighter one much too fast, at about eighty miles-per-hour. He hit a wall on the far side of the road and then bounced back across to the near side. He managed to keep it out of the ditch, otherwise we could easily have been killed.' (Johnny described Volx as the Stoney Middleton of France, and the drive back to Buoux its greatest attraction.)

Not surprisingly for a man in middle age, Ben takes a more thoughtful view of past driving mishaps. 'You change a lot as you get older. I had some great fast cars and I enjoyed them. I'm still into cars and bikes. But now when I see someone driving fast through the streets, especially since I became a father, I look back on what I did and think I'm lucky to be alive.'

In the summer of 1986, Ben spent a lot of time riding his Yamaha out to Water-cum-Jolly's Rubicon Wall, the short curl of white limestone that fringes the artificial pond above Cressbrook Mill. This was the crag Christian Griffith had so disparaged when writing to Ben that year – 'But, really man, Rubicon?' Its proximity to Sheffield and Manchester means Rubicon has had a lot more attention than it might have got in France, and the early and mid 1980s were its heyday. That summer, Tony Ryan climbed the 8a+ *Caviar*, with Ben holding his rope.

With Jerry out of the country and injured, and without having a keen climbing partner readily to hand, Ben would often be at Rubicon on his own, strapping a cassette deck to the motorbike to keep him company while he bouldered out some of Rubicon's notoriously fingery routes. (Ben's musical taste had broadened from hardcore punk, preferring that summer to listen to the more insistent grooves of Isaac Hayes, then in his jazz-funk phase, and Stanley Clarke and his idiosyncratic bass style. He'd even added a couple of Isley Brothers tracks to a mix tape he sent Jerry in Bavaria.) His focus was an unclimbed problem right of *A Miller's Tale*, more a micro-route than pure bouldering given that no one then had bouldering mats, working on the sequence and then jumping off on to the footpath that squeezes between the water's edge and the crag.

'I was trying that problem a lot and had got quite high on it – and was pretty close to doing it. Then I went to Germany and when I came back I heard Chris Gore had done it and put a bolt in it. I was pretty angry, although now I'm not sure why, whether it was because I felt it was my route or because of the bolt. I went down to Rubicon to have a look and Chris was there and I remember having an argument with him, which is when he accused me of being a brat and compared me to Jerry. In retrospect it was nothing.'

Soon after, Ben extended Chris's problem, which Chris had named *Kudos*, into a fully-fledged route and called it *Hot Fun Closing*, the name of a Stanley Clarke track. Two years before Ben had been one of just a handful of British climbers to climb 8a; now it was routine. If Ben was starting to question himself a little, *Hot Fun Closing* wasn't the answer.

Another source of Ben's frustration was knowing he had missed out on a project because he had disappeared to the Frankenjura for a couple of weeks, time he had mostly spent riding motorbikes. Having fun and looning around are part of the appeal of climbing, but not always the best way to get things done. It also helps if you know exactly what it is you want to achieve. And in the summer of 1986, Ben found another alternative to working on hard projects – competition climbing.

The competition circuit is now firmly established and after thirty years its categories and rules are well defined. But the first few years were inevitably fluid and often confusing. Would competitions be acceptable outside? What disciplines would be included? Quite a lot of the world's best climbers were doubtful about the whole project. Initial interest in western Europe was focused in Italy and France, where some of the best climbers, including Patrick Edlinger and Jacky Godoffe, travelled to the Soviet Union to take part in speed-climbing championships. But when France's climbing federation tried to kick start its own version, many leading French climbers publicly declared they were opposed to the whole idea, including the Le Menestrel brothers and Catherine Destivelle, who said: 'I would not participate at any price.' (She then promptly won the first-ever European difficulty event, held in 1985 at Bardonecchia in the Italian region of Piedmont, not far from the French border.)

Bardonecchia was the first event in what was known as the Sportroccia series, the first organised competitions in Europe and a precursor of the current world cup. (In America, bouldering competitions were already established.) These events took place on crags, not walls, and, to the horror of the ethics police, featured routes that were routinely chipped and glued to achieve the correct grade. In one qualifying round, Martin Atkinson pulled off a hold on the route, so the route-setter simply jumared up the rope and drilled another one. At Arco, a stand of trees was chopped down to give spectators a better view, an action publicly criticised by the invited climbers.

Organised by the Italian Alpine Club, Sportroccia events were invitation only, and in 1985 Ben hadn't been invited. That changed the following year, when Ben was part of a strong British contingent, excluding the injured Jerry Moffatt, who showed up for what had now become a two-event series, the first in Arco, near Lake Garda, and the second in Bardonecchia.

Early climbing competitions were notorious for their confused organisation. First there was no isolation zone, so climbers could stand around watching those unlucky enough to go first figuring out the moves. Then, when there was an isolation zone, climbers would get locked up for much of the day, going quietly mad. The sudden presence of commercial interests and sports bureaucrats was not really in the tradition of climbing. On the other hand, Ben loved them, at least initially:

'It was an amazing experience, like you were a superstar. It was nice that people came to watch you, to appreciate what you were doing. It was a real buzz performing in front of thousands of people. What's more, they paid for your travel expenses and accommodation, and that's great when you don't have any money. It was like we were getting some attention. When I turned up at Arco for the first one, Chris [Gore] and Basher

[Martin Atkinson] had been telling everyone that this guy was the man – that he's going to win. No one had ever heard of me. There was huge media interest and I did lots of interviews. They all said to me: "We've heard you're going to win."'

'What did you say?'

'Knowing me, something like: "We'll see how it goes."'

In fact, his first competitions went very well. Scoring in early climbing competitions was often illogical to the point of being nonsensical. You got credit for clipping bolts, not for reaching holds higher than anyone else. At Arco, the climbing on the final route was straightforward up to a roof, where everybody clipped a bolt. Hardly anyone made much progress beyond that point, although Ben did, pulling round its lip to get further than almost anyone else. But he ended up tying with a number of other climbers who hadn't done so well. Despite this, when his scores from both events were added together, he was placed second behind Patrick Edlinger. Had his efforts at Arco been rewarded, he would have finished in first. (Tucked away in letters from his grandfather is a note congratulating him on his performance, a touching link between the 1930s and 1980s.)

After that, with the sudden weight of expectation on him, Ben's performance nose-dived. His next competition, in the late summer of 1987, was at an invitation event at Troubat on the edge of the Pyrenees, laid on by the local climbing club at their crags on the edge of town. This was the first event to combine an on-sight climb with a route competitors could practise, although the climbers were only given half an hour to do this, and then redpoint. Ben's journey down to south-west France had been eventful. The event at Troubat took place a few days after he'd written off his Volkswagen, and since Jerry and Ben Masterson were relying on the lift, Jerry bought an ancient Citroën Dyane, which he remembered as being glacially slow: 'Everything was overtaking us – grannies, wide loads, mobile libraries, everything – but we were having a great time.' Then the brakes failed, just as they approached a red light at a crossroads in rural France.

Ben competing in Europe, around 1991. **Photo:** Ben Moon Collection.

They found a garage, but whatever the mechanic did to fix the brakes had unintended consequences. Drifting through the haze from farmers burning stubble after the harvest, Ben thought he smelt burning. Jerry reassured him it was smoke from the fields.

'No, it's not. I can smell burning rubber and my feet are getting hot. Pull over.'

Lifting the bonnet, a ball of flame roared into the air, so the climbers dived over a wall at the side of the road and waited for the car to explode. When it didn't, they went back for their gear, and then took up their positions behind the wall again. Then, without any warning or explanation, the engine started spontaneously, and the Dyane lurched off down the road, driverless, at a little more than walking pace. The climbers leapt over the wall again and started jogging alongside, flummoxed by what to do next. A truck pulled up and the driver reached in through the Dyane's open window, shoving the gear stick into neutral. Then in a panicked attempt to shut it off, he started pulling wires and tubes out of the burning engine, including the fuel line, which he put in Ben's hands placing Ben's thumb over the end while Jerry took cover. Finally, when the fire was out and the Citröen sat smouldering and broken by the side of the road, they managed to organise a hire car through their insurance and continued south.

That year in Troubat four British climbers were among the final ten battling it out. The French were so amazed at the Brits' showing that they dubbed the final '*L'Heure du Thé*' – teatime. Unfortunately, Ben wasn't one of them. 'There had been no expectations of me the first time,' he says. 'But at Troubat I felt the pressure. I fell off the first qualifying route, about two metres off the ground. I remember actually crying. It was terrible.'

As it turned out, none of the four British finalists made the top three at Troubat and Jerry finished seventh, behind Martin Atkinson and John Dunne. Jerry had expected to find competition climbing to be easy; now he wasn't so sure. From Troubat, they drove to Arco, where Ben did better, finishing tenth, one place behind Jerry and a few places adrift from Chris Gore and Martin Atkinson. It was a chastening experience for both of them.

Ben continued to enter competitions, and enjoyed more success than he did in 1987, but he never managed to shake himself free of his own demons. When Britain staged its first event in Leeds in May 1989, which was also the first World Cup event and endorsed by the world governing body, he was stricken with nerves. This was months after his first ascent of *Agincourt*, at a time when he was regarded as one of the very best rock climbers in the world, and yet: 'Staying in the hotel the night before I was so nervous. I kept waking through the night panicking, and then woke up at first light. I wasn't prepared and it was a total disaster. I went out straight away. I remember that I stuck around for the final, but I don't remember much about it.'

The super-final at Leeds was one of the seminal moments in competition climbing's early history. There had been a lot of scepticism among the old guard of the British climbing establishment about the impact of competitions but almost all of them changed their opinion after an event that was well attended and wholly gripping. Three climbers faced off after reaching the same hold in the final itself. One of them was Jerry Moffatt, who had overcome his own doubts and difficulties to master the discipline. Waiting in the isolation zone, with his two rivals for the title, Simon Nadin and Didier Raboutou, who until that point had proved Jerry's nemesis, Jerry told Didier: 'I'm winning this one today,' before coming out last to flash the route in dramatic style. The contrast with Ben's uncertainty is striking.

'Did it make you question your ability to climb on sight?'

'Yes it did. On-sighting was not my strong suit. But then again, I didn't concentrate on it. I have on-sighted routes up to 8a+, but it wasn't something I worked on much. You need good endurance and the ability to read moves quickly, which you can practise. Working routes and then redpointing them requires a very different technique and mentality. It's a radically different way of going climbing. I was in Buoux in the summer of 1987, and there's no question that competitions sidetracked me from sport climbing. Jerry made the choice between competitions and sport climbing and put his effort into competitions. I went the other way, and focused more on hard sport climbing.'

Compared to Ben, Jerry fed off his sense of competition more readily. Set him a challenge, question his ability, and he would respond. In the spring of 1987, as he began to reach full strength after two years out, Jerry was back at Raven Tor, bouldering and training, with Ben and Ben Masterson, his companions on the road to Troubat that summer. Ben showed Jerry a new boulder problem traverse he had been working on. Ben Masterson then demonstrated some of the moves. Jerry was shocked that he couldn't get anywhere on this sequence, and when he congratulated Masterson, he replied: 'A few things have changed since you've been away.'

'Ben's words were a knife through my heart. In my head I was still the best. And here were two climbers, my old mates, and now they were both burning me off. This was torture.' Within a week, Jerry had mastered the moves, 'still smarting' from Ben Masterson's put-down. Within three weeks, he had completed the whole traverse, something none of the other Raven Tor regulars had managed, and called it *Powerband*, still one of the crag's classic training challenges. After facing injuries that almost ended his career, Jerry wasn't wasting time.

If there was a difference between Ben and Jerry in these years, it was Moffatt's ability to focus on an objective and bend everything in his power towards meeting it. Ben, in his own words, 'wasn't thinking in those terms. I was just climbing, slowly getting better. I certainly didn't consider myself as being one of the best climbers. I didn't see it as my job to push things. I was just trying to find a way to take things on from *Statement*.'

Even his best-known new route from this period, *Zeke the Freak*, 'wasn't a big project. It certainly wasn't world class, not in the way that *Statement* had been. It was possibly the hardest route in the Peak at the time, but that's it.'

The route had a strange and controversial gestation and, as happened with *Kudos*, Ben's absence, this time at the Sportroccia events in Italy in late 1986, almost cost him. Earlier that year, Chris Craggs and Graham Parkes climbed a new aid route on the steep right-hand end of Rubicon and named it *Free That You Bastards!* Since the climb's progenitor is reluctant to discuss it, his motivation can only be guessed at. Perhaps it was intended as a good-humoured challenge to the young sport climbers who had been busily removing points of aid from routes all over Britain. Ben certainly read it as that, which was why he took up the invitation.

By late summer he had, after working the route, managed all the moves and was planning to redpoint the line when his competition debut intervened. During several weeks in Europe, Ben made another trip to Buoux, where he repeated *La Rose et le Vampire*. Antoine Le Menestrel's classically beautiful line is still graded 8b and has a now-famous sequence where the body has to twist and the hands cross through, the left past the right, in an elegant move that seems – and in fact was – deliberately choreographed.

'When I came back to Sheffield, I went out to Rubicon and clipped the first bolt on *Zeke*, felt around for a hold – and it wasn't there. It was gone. The holds had been chipped off.' Ben was furious, 'but then again I didn't do anything about it. I had a go at one of his friends, but he didn't want to say anything.'

Chris Craggs has kept his counsel about this curious event, and did so once again for this book, but his friend and publishing colleague Alan James has commented on why the route was chipped: 'When Ben Moon claimed he had nearly freed the route, Chris went back to take a look. He found lots of chipped holds and chipped them back to what he thought was their natural state.'

One obvious inference from Alan's statement is that Ben chipped holds on *Zeke*, something he categorically dismisses. It would be hard to find a climber from any era who didn't commit some kind of ethical misdemeanour, but Ben's are trivial in any context. In the period immediately before redpointing arrived in Britain, there were countless tales of leading activists finding ways to break those famous unwritten rules. Pete Livesey, who had questioned Ben's use of bolts on *Statement of Youth*, had resorted several times to improving holds to climb routes. Others used tricks to sneak rests, such as jamming a foot against the rope with it clipped in above you, essentially giving a top rope, and other such ruses.

In Europe, chipping holds was commonplace. Many of the most popular routes at Buoux were only made possible by either drilling or gluing on holds. Antoine Le Menestrel did both on *La Rose et le Vampire*, including its famous cross-through sequence. *Tabou Zizi* was notorious for having drilled holes for finger pockets, which had to be located precisely and were painful to climb.

'We thought it was strange,' says Ben. 'But people do things differently in different countries. They have so much rock there and they didn't value the rock in the same way. Here it's more limited.' (The counterargument was that routes could be, like works of art, created to be pleasurable and accessible, hence *La Rose*. Marc Le Menestrel would later recant this sort of creativity: 'With chipping and gluing, the routes will come down to the level that people can do, and there will be no progress.')

Yet to suggest Ben might have chipped a route to get a first ascent is really to misjudge the British sport-climbing project in general and his career in particular. Ben was already heading down a path where incremental increases in difficulty were the objective, not producing lots of new climbs for the sake of it or even climbing the last great lines still available. The total number of routes he put up is low, certainly compared to leading climbers from previous generations. So there wasn't much logic in chipping a route to bring it down to a grade he was already capable of climbing.

'I've never chipped a hold, or glued a hold on. I've never tried to rationalise why; I just never did it. Maybe someone told me when I was starting that it was wrong. It does seem pointless. It defeats the object.' (Ben freely confesses to two ethically impure acts in his climbing career, one occasion early on when his rope became jammed in a crack while climbing *Groove of Horror* at Tremadog with Steve Lewis, letting him rest without his second realising it – 'Man, I was so pumped!'; and stepping on a peg while climbing the route that had given him so much trouble at Buoux, *Fissure Serge*. He blushes when he admits all this, and then laughs at himself for doing so.)

Ben completed his project at Rubicon in August 1987, figuring out another sequence of moves to the left of the original aid line, and called it *Zeke the Freak*, after an Isaac Hayes track. (As was still routine, it got an English grade, E8 6c.) A beautiful, dappled shot of Ben taken by Richie Brooks was the first cover of the newly launched *On The Edge* magazine, the first but not the last time he appeared on a cover. As one of the best 8bs in the Peak District, it's become a popular milestone over the years, still a route where the best can calibrate their progress, although as holds have snapped off, its grade has fluctuated a little. Thanks to the internet, even if you can't climb it yourself, it's possible to watch others do so. It's a typical Rubicon route, requiring brutally strong fingers and, although short, the complexity of the moves is incredible as suitors contort their bodies to keep their fingers on the holds.

But while it was a significant landmark for him personally, and was certainly one of the hardest routes in Britain at the time, *Zeke* hadn't pushed boundaries. Ben was still playing catch up with the best sport climbers in Europe – Wolfgang Güllich, the Le Menestrel brothers and Jibé Tribout. In the next two years that would change, but it would take a strange catalyst to propel Ben into the lead.

He broke his arm.

Agincourt: the first ascent. **Photos**: Chris Plant.

AGINCOURT

Sport is littered with stories of great talents never fully realised, of prodigiously gifted youths whose potential remained just that. What is it that allows one to prosper and a hundred others to fall away? Unless you're actively involved with sport at an elite level, it's easy to underestimate the intensity of the mental pressure you face, of training for month after month, wondering all the time if you'll succeed, and if you do, whether it's worth it. In the mid to late 1980s, climbers were facing these issues for the first time in the sport's history.

Jasper Sharpe, one of the best sport climbers from the generation that immediately followed Ben, wrote a powerful description on the website *ukbouldering.com* about his aspirations as a young climber and why he hadn't achieved all that he might have done:

'Looking back at when I stopped climbing I think if you look at the boys from my generation who were supremely talented and should have gone on to push standards forward it's interesting that **nobody** did. Malcolm [Smith] made his mark with doing *Hubble* when he did (and obviously bouldering hard) but we felt then that that was just the start.

'So why didn't it work out like that? In a word, I reckon, money. Needing it, wanting it or just plain having to go out and earn it has restricted the best climbers of my generation from reaching their potential … Perhaps we should have been able to just continue. You can't expect something for nothing. Appreciate the fact that you can't make a living from **just** being good at a minority sport. But the fact is that we all thought that the money was there to be earned if we just climbed hard enough and at 18 when all you want to do is climb for the rest of your life and you see Jerry driving a Porsche (and you've just burned him off at the Tor) you assume it will come. Life's simple at 18.'

Had Ben been more motivated by material concerns, then the frustrations of living on very little and trying to perform as a world-class athlete might have been too much for him to bear. Plenty of Olympic athletes from minority sports are heard bemoaning a lack of funding as an explanation for why they didn't achieve as much as they might have. Apart from a weakness for motorbikes and fast cars, which he indulged later, when his profile grew along with his sponsorship deals, for much of his career he lived an essentially ascetic life, sustained by the dole and miniscule sponsorship deals.

His first deal, aged nineteen, was simply a little cash to fund a trip to Buoux, given to him by Dick Turnbull, then marketing director at climbing hardware company Wild Country. On that trip, in late 1985, Ben made the third ascent of *Chouca* – the steeply overhanging line of pockets first climbed by Marc Le Menestrel. It gave him a buzz to see the photos of him climbing it used by Wild Country as a poster. The route became almost iconic, partly because of a radical solution to a long reach off a deep pocket that required climbers to slot a leg through an elbow – the peculiar figure-of-four move. (Marc, determined that every climber got the full force of his creation, would routinely clear the small pile of boulders that would grow under *Chouca* like a stony mushroom to help climbers past the first fierce pull on to the route.)

It was probably these occasional appearances in advertising campaigns that caught the attention of more mainstream media. In the autumn of 1986 he got a letter from the journalist Neil Spencer, who as editor of the *New Musical Express* had written the first review of a Sex Pistols gig and was now working on a new magazine called *Arena*. Spencer wanted to include a specially commissioned photo of Ben in the magazine's first edition, shot by Eamonn McCabe, then one of the country's leading sports photographers and later picture editor for *The Guardian*.

Arena, before it morphed into a low-rent men's magazine, was a style bible that introduced the concept of the 'new man' and for a few years set the agenda for the national press when it came to all things fashionable. A superbly fit, good-looking athlete with a wild set of dreads and an edgy attitude doing something left-of-field like rock climbing was too good to resist. It seems Britain's taste gurus understood how climbing's appeal was changing before the sport itself did.

Older commentators were not alone in mourning the fact that climbing was moving from being a counter-cultural lifestyle to a professionalised sport, with all that implies: sponsors, training, nutrition, managing injuries and hanging on to the self-belief that you're good enough. Wolfgang Güllich himself regretted the way things were going: 'Climbing is becoming a reflection of society, climbers' image of themselves as part of an alternative culture is changing to the ideology of the dominant concept of sport. Commerce and the media are affecting what happens.'

It's certainly true that from the 1980s onwards climbing became much more consumerist. It was now possible for a few savvy rock climbers, and not just mountaineers, to make a living from their chosen sport. But just as with mountaineering, it was generally those who were not only capable on rock but good communicators as well – people who understood what the climbing public wanted to see and read, and what would resonate with sponsors and the media. (Ben posed the question, somewhat artlessly, in an interview with Gill Kent at *On The Edge* magazine: 'Is Jerry really worth £20,000 more than me?')

'I hadn't really twigged that you had to get out and promote yourself,' Ben says. 'I probably got better at it, but when I was young I assumed that if you did hard things, then the media would come to you. They'd notice and write things. But it didn't work like that, probably still doesn't. You get really talented climbers, but you never hear anything about them. Kids these days are media savvy. They can video themselves and reach the public without the intervention of the media.'

The climbing press might have ignored Ben but he was interviewed not long after climbing *Zeke* for a BBC radio documentary called *Hard Fire Inside*, presented by Sheffield writer Dave Sheasby, a regular contributor to Radio 4, but usually as a scriptwriter. (He used the experience to write a radio play about a journalist trying to get a story from a group of rock climbers holding a wake for a friend who has fallen to his death.) For his contribution, Ben got a cheque for £20.

More lucrative were the small sponsorship deals that came his way as his profile grew in climbing competitions. After his success at Bardonecchia in 1986, Ben got a lift home from Italy with the importer of Asolo boots and they agreed a deal for him to wear their rock shoes for £1,000 a year. There were also appearance fees for competitions, something that boosted their appeal for young climbers in the early days. Later, when the British Mountaineering Council became involved, there was some financial support for the World Cup series. (Ben would have his knuckles rapped in a stiff letter from the BMC after he was photographed at an informal bouldering competition at Crookrise in the early 1990s. Competitions were by then a purely indoor phenomenon, on pain of suspension.)

None of this adds up to very much at all, barely enough to keep body and soul together. Of course, there was nothing new in this. Climbers have been living like vagrants for decades right back into the 1930s when the sport's patrician social background began to be diluted. Plenty of other climbers were living on next to nothing in the 1980s. But few of them were training and climbing with the same intensity and the same focus on technical performance. Many of those Ben came across while climbing assumed the well-spoken, privately educated Londoner had a trust fund or an allowance to keep him going, as some of his peers did, but he was more or less on his own.

'I remember he was posh and had a Sony Walkman,' one northern contemporary recalled. 'I think I probably nicked it,' Ben says. Later, when he had several small sponsorship deals, the next impoverished generation thought him wealthy.

Some of the older generation had dismissed sport climbers as soulless machines with half an eye on what they could make from it. But all Ben was interested in was climbing. 'You don't do it for money,' Ben says. 'You've got to have a passion for what you're doing. If you're waking up in the morning and you hate the idea of going climbing then you're going to struggle. When you do feel unmotivated you have to knuckle down and work. Climbing was its own reward. Nobody would do the Tour de France after the first year unless they were paid for it. Climbing is different from cycling or running because it feels so varied. There are so many different kinds, so many different rock types. It's a way of life. More money wouldn't have made much difference to me. The compensation was laughable in comparison to the commitment.'

Up to this point, climbers had been solving problems on crags as they were presented to them. But as standards rose, that became more difficult. Ben now had moves in his head that he was struggling to find on rock. 'That was certainly true in the UK,' he says. 'The rock's limited. You need the right amount of holds, hard enough that it's worthwhile, easy enough that you can do it. That's why the hardest routes are so long. It's easier to find a 9b that's thirty metres long, than the 9b equivalent of *Hubble*.'

In this he had something in common with Johnny Dawes, who was able to abstract shapes and problems from the rock in front of him – and imagine moves before he found them. The difference between them, superficially anyway, was Johnny's intolerance of what he regarded as a pedantic attachment to training and focus, preferring movement and change – and his appetite for danger. Uncertainty was the spice of his life and without it climbing didn't make quite so much sense. ('Where was the drama?' he complained, describing the climbing in Buoux as 'painful and awkward'. He posed the question: 'Can it make people like that?')

'It's not possible, to pin it down to one thing,' Ben says. 'Why you choose one form of climbing over another. The buzz you get from bold climbing has something to do with it. Johnny's physique wasn't suited to sport climbing. I would say that made it harder for him. Mine probably is and you tend to go for the things you're good at. Having said that, there's no reason why I couldn't have gone for bolder climbing. Maybe I'm a bit of a coward? I have done some bold climbs. But like anything, you've got to apply yourself to it. I chose not to because I actively preferred sport climbing. Spending that first summer with all those guys at Pen Trwyn probably had a big effect. I was fresh out of school, these were my heroes, and it was all about climbing as hard as you could. I became friends with Jerry and went to France, just as the whole sport-climbing revolution was happening. It set a pattern. If that hadn't happened, and I'd been with other people who were climbing trad all the time, maybe I would have gone down that route.'

In the late 1980s, Ben and Johnny spent a lot of time together, particularly at Buoux and then later when Johnny lived for a while in Ben's house. Johnny took Ben up to the Outer Hebrides with Paul Pritchard to climb a new E6 called *Mosskil Grooves* on the looming, damp bulk of Sron Ulladale on the Isle of Harris. ('At the base was a wet mica slab, which we cautioned him against,' Johnny wrote in his memoirs. 'He went straight across it like a well-seasoned shuffler.') Ben – calm, laconic – enjoyed the creative mayhem that Johnny trailed behind himself, like a cloak, knocking things over. 'He's fun to be around; the flip side are the mood swings. We are,' he adds drily, 'very different people.' Those differences in personality are revealed to an extent in their different approaches to climbing.

Interviewed after his first ascent of *Agincourt*, he was asked whether it was possible to excel at both traditional and sport climbing. 'You can't do both well,' he concluded. 'They're not compatible.' Twenty-five years on,

L–R, Paul Pritchard, Ben and Johnny Dawes below Sron Ulladale. **Photo:** Gordon Stainforth.

he still feels the same way. 'The reward of risk is the buzz but the climbing is not so technically difficult. The psychological effort is keeping it together in the face of risk. It's an immediate reward. The rewards of sport climbing require months and years of sustained training.'

Perhaps, ultimately, it is a question of taste, not ethics, of preferring a David Hockney to a Lucian Freud – or a Jeremy Moon.

What Johnny and Ben did have in common was a passion for speed. The filmmaker Alun Hughes, working on their film *Stone Monkey*, remembers travelling to Manchester from Sheffield in the back seat of Johnny's

Peugeot along the sinuous line of the Snake Pass, Ben's eyes like saucers as Johnny worked up and down the gears, thinking through the tyres. Johnny introduced Ben to the boulder problems he'd done on the concrete supports for the Mancunian Way. Lay-backing tenuously up a slick arête, in November 1987, Ben's foot skidded off; he put out his right hand to break his fall and broke instead the scaphoid bone in his wrist.

It was a bad break, and Ben spent the next four months with his arm in plaster. Unable to climb, he enrolled on a literature course at a further education college, Granville College. 'I spent a lot of the time reading: Charlotte Brontë, Dickens, Shakespeare, Graham Greene's *The Power and the Glory*. I loved it, reading these books and talking about them, but we had to write essays and do short exams. That was horrendous. It was five years since I left Christ's Hospital to go climbing, and I was never very good at school anyway. I looked around the room and everyone had their heads down.'

Christian Griffith wrote to him from Colorado, commiserating at his bad luck and illustrating the letter with a cartoon showing how the weight of his dreadlocks might have caused the accident. Christian was always direct and open in his letters and didn't hesitate to mix some advice with the sympathy: 'You're a bright person Ben, but it seems like you can also be lazy and lack motivation. But I think school is really worth hanging in there. Since I graduated I've done very little with my degree but being well educated by itself I think is valuable.'

Ben rolls his eyes at the notion he was lazy, but there's no question that these four months off climbing were an opportunity to take stock and plan for the future. In late 1987 he moved into a new flat on William Street, to live on his own, before going to Kingston for Christmas. Living on his own was a marked and deliberate change from the years of communal living, and signified a moment when he began to be more focused. In early January he was back in Sheffield putting the flat in order and considering his next move in a letter to his mother and sister:

'A few years must have passed by since you last received a letter from me. Plenty of postcards but no letters … My wrist is aching a little; I had the plaster removed on Friday morning. All things considered, if what the doctor said was true, then it feels fairly good. The doctor said it was bound to ache when moved in a vertical direction, since it had been im-mobilised for ten weeks. I hope he is right!'

The bulk of the letter wasn't about his recovery, but about taking control of how he was living and arrangements for the future: 'On Wednesday I have an interview to see whether I am eligible for becoming self-employed which I am, [since] several of my friends having done a similar thing already. This will mean that I am able to earn some money while still receiving dole and rent, and will also allow me to go abroad. Previously this was illegal. This probably all sounds very easy to you. I suppose it is. It's called the Enterprise Allowance Scheme.'

The value of this attempt by Margaret Thatcher's government to encour-age the unemployed to set up their own businesses is debatable. Tracy Emin and the editors of *Viz* magazine relied on it when they were starting out, but you suspect they would have got there in the end without it. For Ben, it was more useful than you might suppose. 'The thing that kept me going was the Enterprise Allowance Scheme. You didn't have to sign on and there was a bit more money. You also had to produce a business plan and keep basic accounts, that sort of thing. It was good practice.'

Some climbers have publicly regretted pursuing their sport at the tax-payer's expense, but Ben is more equivocal. 'I do a little now that I'm older. When they're debating benefits on the radio, which they do a lot now, I sometimes feel I'm getting a little more right wing, but basically it doesn't worry me. The dole was my degree. Climbing was growing, and the dole allowed me to climb, get better and then commercialise my sport. You could say I was training for a profession.'

The pitfalls of that profession were expertly laid out in a second letter from Christian Griffith that winter, a typical illustration of what happens when a passion for climbing meets the realities of business: 'We must have formed a special friendship after almost killing each other over that pear [Ben has no recollection of the pear incident]. I am sorry to hear about your arm's extended stay in the pot. What a drag that must be. Socialised medicine sounds pretty sketchy man. It's also too bad you've been having a hard time with sponsors but in a way there can't be anything wonderful about that whole business. It seemed a bit to me that the people who get so deeply involved in it either become unfriendly, tight [and] insecure businessmen or else they become like scavengers, happy at whatever bones are thrown their way. As you can probably guess I have been struggling with that whole scene myself. America moneywise is of course far worse and the companies don't really make any attempt at establishing relationships with leading climbers. I used to get so frustrated about the whole thing but in retrospect I am glad it is like that. It has no pretences. It doesn't suck you in and get you comfortable. Personally, I have a very hard time extending my dream to the working social world. Normally when I feel I have figured something out I take a very uncompromising command of my pursuit of it and in business I hate all the effort one has to go to, to penetrate the morass of all the mindless people who have been forced to give up their dreams and are going to do their damned best to make sure you do too. For a while there I was playing with the idea of design. I had done some with karabiners, buckles, boots, clothing etc. I had even gotten some good part-time work doing drawings for Lowe and some of my designs may even get picked up but companies move so painfully slow, ideas become so anonymous and ultimately everything is reduced to money. I am questioning if I was right in thinking that you could make money climbing and still enjoy the sport. I am going to try and hang in there and see what happens but if the signs are not a hundred per cent I will escape! But I should stop and give you some news ... '

Now twenty-one, the realities of life were beginning to filter into Ben's existence. Contemporaries at school would soon be graduating from

Martin 'Basher' Atkinson and Ben in France. **Photo:** Ben Moon Collection.

university and starting their careers. Already some of the climbers he'd hung out with at Pen Trwyn a few years before had quit full-time climbing and got jobs. In the summer of 1988, Martin Atkinson would finish his longstanding project at Raven Tor and next day head for Switzerland and a job with outdoor gear company Mammut. He called the route *Mecca: the Midlife Crisis*, the first in Britain to be graded 8b+. He was twenty-six. Martin would have been happy to carry on climbing. 'With the climbing contracts I had at the time I could survive and have a reasonable life: buy a house, run a car, take a holiday and most importantly climb.' It was fear of the future that persuaded him to take the job. 'A serious accident or injury would have left me without an income or career.'

If life was beginning to seem a little more complicated than dossing in caves in North Wales, or hitching to France, Ben did at least have one major stroke of luck. A relative in Canada, Ruth's brother-in-law, died, and left his estate to her children. Because Jeremy had died, his share went to his children. Ben would inherit a sizeable chunk of money, enough to buy a small terraced house just off Abbeydale Road for £19,000. With a little rental income and – as he slowly learned his own value and his profile rose in Britain – better sponsorship deals, he would find himself pretty much in the position Martin Atkinson described. This was all a little in the future. For now, in his letter to his mother, he broached the subject of a short-term loan, to be repaid when his legacy came through, so he could immediately buy himself 'a good, reliable and practical car.'

In a new flat, with plans laid for the future, Ben went to work on his injured wrist, recovering his strength in a matter of weeks. He packed his books from his literature course and headed for the south of France, his life falling back into a familiar pattern: late winter and autumn in Buoux, summers in the Peak District and some competitions in between. Something, however, had changed. Up to this point, Ben had been half a step behind the world's best. He had been the front-runner in that larger group who come agonisingly close, who come within a fraction of taking the final step – but don't. Perhaps the months spent away from climbing had made him understand that patiently waiting for something to happen wasn't enough. If he was going to realise his potential, then the time to act was now.

Over the course of the next two years, Ben would overtake pretty much all those ahead of him to become the leading sport climber in the world – and it began almost immediately. Just six weeks after his hand came out of plaster, he did a sequence of three of the hardest routes at Buoux in a matter of days: *Le Spectre du Sur-mutant* on the Monday, *Le Minimum* on the Friday and the route he'd come so close on in 1986, *La Rage de Vivre*, on the following Wednesday. In just nine days he'd despatched the work of France's best three sport climbers: in order, Jibé Tribout, Marc Le Menestrel and Antoine Le Menestrel. Only Jerry Moffatt had, by that stage, climbed all three of these routes.

'I have now been here just under three weeks,' Ben wrote to his brother Rob. 'So far the trip has been a success. The main purpose of coming to Buoux was to recover the fitness and strength that I lost during my three-month layoff. Although I am still considerably down on pure power, I am climbing far better than I imagined I would be ... As for my schoolwork, although I came prepared with all my books I haven't managed a word. I can't really see myself going back to college because I don't think I will have the time.'

With the perspective of time, Ben says: 'I came back with a different head on after my injury. Those were probably the three hardest routes in the world at the time. [*Le Spectre* and *La Rage* are now graded 8b+; *Le Minimum* is now 8c.] I was really fit and strong and incredibly motivated. I remember shortly afterwards bumping into Jerry somewhere, and all he could say was that he couldn't believe it. It wasn't "well done" or "good effort"; he just couldn't believe it.' If there was a moment when Ben stepped out from Jerry's shadow, this was it.

A few weeks later, Ben was in the Frankenjura with Sean Myles and the Belgian climber Arnould t'Kint. After doing a quick repeat of an 8a+ put up by Wolfgang Güllich, Ben wondered aloud whether it was worth the grade. 'Arnie said no, that it really was 8a+. That I was now one of the top five in the world.'

'What did you say?'

'Who are the other four?'

Having now done everything he wanted to at Buoux, the next logical step was to find something new, something harder – something to move the game on. Most of the hardest routes at Buoux, like *La Rage* and *Le Minimum*, are at Le Bout du Monde – the end of the world. But Ben knew about a line next to *Le Spectre*, at a section of the crag called

Les Dévers, or the slopes – and not sloping in a good way. Laurent Jacob had re-equipped an old aid line called *Les Barouilles* – meaning 'bolts' – and Marc Le Menestrel had given it a try but after a brief campaign decided it was too hard.

'He could have done it,' Ben says. 'They were both very good. Marc was maybe a little stronger, Antoine a bit more natural. He was also more quiet and thoughtful, very artistic and creative. He would choose operas as route names. It's not surprising to me that he's a dancer now; or that Marc is a lecturer at top business schools. Marc is more extroverted, a bit of a showman, a bit arrogant. I really like him a lot. Marc and Patrick Edlinger were similar in that way – big personalities.'

Ben moved into his new house that summer, and in the autumn headed back to Buoux to lay siege to his new project. There was often a clutch of the world's best climbers at the crag in those years, but late 1988 turned out to be unusually vibrant. Ben rented a caravan with Jerry Moffatt. Johnny Dawes shared a leaky tent with Sean Myles until the first bad weather, and then moved into the caravan. Always struggling with the intense discipline sport climbing dictated, Ben recalls him 'getting into really good shape – toned and ripped and very light. He had a good go at sport climbing and did some quite hard routes.'

Dawes recalled the mood in the caravan: 'Sandpaper grinds away splits in skin, topos, half-used oval vitamin E pills perch on the aluminium rim of double-glazing cloaked in condensation.' Johnny, never more than half-sold on the sport-climbing project, was an adroit observer of the talent on show: 'I remember Didier 'Rambo' Raboutou, Jerry's diminutive nemesis on the competition circuit, would warm up in white gloves. When he had done enough he would do a final stretch of his hands and announce 'Didier is ready!' and have his sexy girlfriend peel them off.'

While Johnny got into shape and worked up through the grades, Ben focused intensely on the project at Les Dévers. 'I spent a long time on it, seventeen or eighteen days over a couple of months, October and

Agincourt. **Photo:** Takashi Nakagawa.

November 1988.' The route has fourteen separate moves on it; two, perhaps three of them are English 7a and the rest are 6c, all on a wildly overhanging wall. Every time he moved a hand, he had to hit the next hold, usually a poor pocket, absolutely right. Every body position, every tenuous dink for his feet, all of it had to be precisely timed and executed and he had to believe that it could be done, that he was good enough and strong enough. The famous image of him hanging from two poor pockets halfway to a crucifix position says it all.

The route didn't even reach the top of the crag, but stopped halfway up the wall at a couple of large pockets where Ben could get a hands-off rest. By the late 1980s that wasn't unusual, but it was still controversial. 'It just wasn't relevant to us,' Ben says. 'If you do a sequence of hard climbing and then get to a jug where you can hang out all day, you may as well stop the route there.'

The patience and concentration, let alone the physical effort, began to take its toll on Ben as the pressure to finish the route became more intense with each passing day. He told Georgina in a long letter about the challenge he was facing and how he had decided to stay longer than originally planned: 'I remember when I used to go away climbing that I tended to feel homesick after about two and a half weeks. Now four weeks goes by as if it were a fortnight.'

He no longer sees being in France as being on holiday he tells his sister. He's come to do a job: 'As for my climbing, that's going pretty well with nothing really to complain about especially now I'm on my all fruit diet! When I was last here, I don't know if you remember, but there were three particular routes I wanted to do and did. These were probably the hardest in the world and didn't leave me anything else to do here except a new route, which is what I'm doing now and will be, I think I can safely say, (if I'm allowed to) the hardest in the world. French grade 8c, which, if that means nothing to you, I am sure Robert will explain.'

He'd go to sleep at night going through the sequence of moves in his head and wake up on the morning of a redpoint attempt rehearsing them again. ('My memory for moves is really bad,' he once told an interviewer. 'I don't learn things. My good point is my power. I think a lot of other climbers lack a lot in that respect.' The second part may be true, but not the first. Almost a quarter of a century on, his hands can still move through at least some of the moves.)

More than three weeks after his letter he wrote to Georgina again, and the frustration was now palpable. He is, he writes, listening to Womack & Womack in the caravan – *Teardrops*, presumably – to stave off the boredom of a rest day. 'If I do it, I'm buying all my friends a meal. I very much want to go home now having been out here for seven weeks. Too long a time. I'm looking forward to Christmas at [Mum's] and seeing you and Rob.'

He would climb for a few days, with a sequence of patient belayers – Chris Plant, Mark Pretty, Andy Goring – take a rest day, followed by a lighter climbing day and then another rest day. 'That was the pattern we figured out for ourselves. We found that system better than two straight rest days. You felt light and strong after that.' Jerry had been experimenting with losing weight while training in Germany the winter before, eating an omelette a day and working out on Wolfgang Güllich's Campus board. 'After that, Zippy, Sean and I went on a similar diet for about a week. But I couldn't really see where I could lose weight. I've never had to diet. At eighteen I'd been 9st 3lb. Back then, when I was trying *Agincourt*, I was about 10st. My weight has always stayed the same. I did record it for a bit, but it never changed so I stopped bothering. The most weight I ever lost was when my dreads were cut off.'

In retrospect Ben had spent too long in France. 'More than a six-week trip is too much sport climbing. You start to lose it. I had a circuit on the Styx Wall, to get warmed up for *Agincourt*, including a fingery 7b. I remember floating up it for weeks and then suddenly one day falling off. I remember crying. I was so burned out. I just thought "I'm never going to do this". When you're climbing well it all comes naturally, it's all easy. At other times it's desperate – and that can all happen on the same route.'

In a postcard he sent Rob from Fontainebleau in the late autumn of 1989: 'I don't know when I'm coming back but we'll be going back down south in five days for a little longer. You don't really envy me. I really am fed up with the south of France, the reasons being too many to list here; ask me later. My motivation is so up and down at the moment, it's horrible. Trying to do hard routes in France just doesn't allow for this. You have to be fully motivated all of the time. One of my main problems is that I met the lovely Czech girl at the competition in Nuremberg and I am now paying for it. Tell you all about it when I see you.'

'Did you ever think you'd spent too much time at Buoux overall?'

'Yeah, maybe. But it was the hub of everything then. Those were the hardest routes in the world.'

Apart from Jerry and Johnny, there were a lot of friends from the British climbing scene visiting Buoux, and plenty of leading sport climbers from other countries too. He began friendships that have lasted ever since, and the climbers who saw what he and others were doing became ambassadors, bringing home news from the court of the sport-climbing gods to those far-flung corners of Europe and North America still adjusting to the revolution. Jim Karn and Scott Franklin, two of America's early-adopters were there, and Christian Griffith too. When it came time for him to leave, with Ben still toiling to finish his project, Christian gave him a new-fangled energy food to help him on his way: 'This will get you up the route,' he said. 'It's called a PowerBar.'

It almost worked. He got to the last move of the route but fell before completing it. Ben went home to Kingston for Christmas to see his family with the project unfinished, and then spent some time bouldering on gritstone in the Peak District. It seemed to do the trick. 'In the new year I went back to Buoux and did the route really quickly, after one or two tries.' *Statement of Youth* had been a landmark climb in its way, but this new climb was something else. Debates about whether or not it was the first 8c in the world have somewhat overshadowed the route's impact, illustrating that an obsession with grades can go too far. Taken in context with his first ascent of *Maginot Line*, which he completed soon after and also rated 8c, Ben had clearly moved into the front rank of sport climbers. These were well-known projects at the epicentre of the sport-climbing revolution, and the small but intensely competitive group who were capable of understanding what Ben had done were impressed. *Maginot Line* had been a project for several leading French climbers, most notably Alex Duboc. Its putative name was *Le Plafond*, which appeared on a small plaque at the base of the cliff. When Ben climbed it, Patrick Edlinger took the plaque down and ceremoniously handed it to Ben.

His choice of route names was, as he acknowledges, provocative. At the suggestion of Sean Myles, he called the Buoux route *Agincourt – Azincourt* in French – as a cheeky dig at beating the French at their own game in their

Maginot Line. **Photo**: Takashi Nakagawa.

own home. The joke backfired a little, causing annoyance, even offence, to some. When five years later Jibé Tribout extended *Maginot Line* to join the existing route *Terminator* to create an 8c+, he called the route *La Lune dans le Caniveau* – the moon in the gutter – before it reverted to the less contentious *Superplafond*. 'He should have stuck with it,' Ben said. 'It was a good response.'

His route names and his habit of speaking his mind to journalists with direct, even combative answers, was sometimes perplexing for journalists. Jack Moon, reading an interview with Ben a few years later in *On The Edge*, wrote to him: 'I read your interview in *OTE* with much interest – and appreciated the final paragraph. It reads well, suggests you have a touch of acid in your blood, which doesn't suffer fools gladly; which you have inherited from Jeremy, and he from me! It comes from my mother's side of the family, and one can't escape one's inheritance.' For French journalists, used to French climbers, who talk more readily about the aesthetic, or how they feel, or what inspires them, it was baffling. The writer Vincent Albrand, described Ben as 'not being afraid to provoke, to say what he thinks,' and noted his willingness to mount 'a crusade' against those – coincidentally, as it happened – French climbers overstating the grades of their climbs.

Writing a few years after the first ascent of *Agincourt*, Albrand was intrigued, even confused at how Ben projected himself. 'It's a paradox. At home, he's an agreeable lad, open, self-effacing (although less so towards midnight) … a true gentleman. Hard to imagine that this smiling young man across the table from me will, a few moments later, transform himself into a serial killer of hard routes, shredding a set of Michelin tyres on the narrow lanes of the Peak District, tearing up the dance floor, or something similar. This split in personality is a peculiarly British habit. You can only really understand the English when they're excited about something … arrogant, temperamental, bitter or just simply honest and passionate? It's up to you to decide. But he deserves your attention.'

In the course of a lengthy interview, Albrand asks Ben whether his route names *Agincourt* and *Maginot Line* had been a declaration of war. 'No,' he replied. 'It wasn't meant to be aggressive. It was just a little joke, because those battles were fought on French territory – nothing nasty. I apologise if anybody was upset. It's an English habit, to wind people up a little, especially the French.' Over the years, Ben has become more apologetic. 'Maybe it was in bad taste naming a route after a battle where all those people died. Looking back, now that I'm older, I do feel a bit guilty.'

The French, Albrand wrote, had been unfairly indifferent to Ben, despite his exceptional achievements. But the French press, whatever their criticisms of his blunt attitude and provocative route names, gave him plenty of attention. The reaction at home to becoming the first British climber to put up routes of such intense difficulty was muted. *On The Edge* at least sensed the scale of what he'd done. The magazine ran a short article by Ben with an account of *Maginot Line*, which opened with Takashi Nakagawa's stunning shot of him – printed across two pages – hanging from poor pockets on *Agincourt*, his feet off, face set in an agonised grimace, as though hanging from a cross. 'I know this might sound arrogant,' he famously wrote, 'but 6c is just not that hard any longer, and 6b is approaching a rest.' *High* magazine ran a short interview with him after *Agincourt*, but it was close friend Sean Myles asking the questions and the piece began: 'Ben Moon has always been a mysterious character in this country.' If a British climber put up the hardest route in the world now, you sense the reaction would be a little more fulsome.

Could he see himself, Sean asked, climbing 9a? 'No,' Ben replied. 'I'll be over the hill by then. Maybe 8c+ though. I don't know how many years I've got in me. It's a problem of finding the routes.' It must have seemed incredible to ordinary climbers that there was so little rock left in the world that Ben Moon was having trouble finding something to climb, but it's a problem the world's top climbers would increasingly face – the ephemeral line between a route that is the hardest but still possible.

He would have to come home to find it.

Ben working the *Whore of Babylon*, the bottom of which would later become *Hubble*. **Photo:** Ben Moon Collection.

HUBBLE

Ben puts down his cup of espresso and from memory explains how to climb *Hubble*, in 1990 the hardest sport route in the world. 'You start on a little flake below the overlap and make a big span to a pinch.' Sitting upright in his chair, his left hand shoots out and I can see his legs straining as a memory map of the climb starts to boss his mind around. 'That's not a very hard move. You get a right heel-hook underneath the roof and go up for a small three-finger undercut.' The fingers of his right hand invert and pinch themselves together. The hold isn't just small, it's hostile and unaccommodating, like a waiter in a Paris restaurant. He has to build his body over it before he can take full advantage.

'So that's the start of the crux. You've got to get your feet up round the roof on that. The crux move is holding that undercut to get a two-finger pocket, which is hard to fit your fingers inside and be precise. Then you've got to move your feet, snatch up for a sloping three-finger edge, get a toe-hook behind the pinch you had at the start, come in for another three-finger under-cling, release the toe-hook, stand up and slap for a layaway shoulder press and then slap again for a flat hold. Then you've got a jug.' He pauses for a moment, not for effect, just to run this sequence through his head. Then he says: 'All of those moves are hard.'

Watching the sequence on video, catching the pocket happens at waist level and looks awkward rather than desperate. Yet the speed at which his hand flicks into place shows just how marginal this move really is.

He adjusts his fingers inside it, then reaches up and right, and his body sinks down on that three-finger edge, arm extending as it takes his weight, fingers crimped on almost nothing with his thumb locked across them, working his feet round. Now he can slap into that crushingly powerful shoulder press, flipping his hand around so that it smacks into the rock, before crouching slightly and going again with his right hand for the better hold.

'*Hubble* is seven hand moves long,' he says. 'Each move of the hand or foot is hard. It's not a question of get a hold and then move.' All the slight adjustments he makes on the route make it look like he's in pain, trying to get comfortable, as though the rock is hot and he can barely touch it, that it is spitting him off. Shorn of context, names and grades, the where and the what, you know instinctively that this is someone at the limit of what's possible for them, someone in their element. When psychologists talk about self-actualisation, this is what it looks like.

The reaction this sequence of climbing got in Britain was, in comparison to *Agincourt's* reception the previous year, instantaneous and fulsome. 'World's hardest route crosses Channel – now resident at Raven Tor,' was the headline in *High* magazine's Rock Notes, now edited by Neil Foster who had proved one of the more even-handed observers from this period. That crux move, he told readers, was in Ben's reckoning English 7b and the following three moves were 7a. This was a boggling level of difficulty to most British climbers. 'We were still a little bit on the English grading system,' Ben says. 'I gave it E9/10 7a, I think, and talked about there being a 7b move. There probably is if *Revelations* is 7a. We were definitely a lot more cautious with grading in those days. I never thought of giving it 9a. We really felt that a grade was divided into three: bottom end, middle and hard. If you're climbing at your limit, a tiny bit of extra difficulty can feel like a huge difference but it's not necessarily a whole grade up. 8c+ seemed a massive jump from 8c. I never thought of going further.'

It was clear to Ben that he had done something that was, in Neil Foster's words, 'in a quite different league of difficulty to either of [his] French routes, hence its grade of 8c+, the first time this standard has been claimed and, according to Ben, undoubtedly the hardest route in the world at this present time.' Ben remembers being more equivocal than that. 'I knew it was hard. I knew it was the hardest piece of climbing I'd done, and by quite a long way. But you don't know that someone else isn't doing something equally hard elsewhere.'

On the other hand, he did know that they weren't doing something equally hard at Buoux. With the completion of *Agincourt*, there wasn't anything else for Ben to do there and his successes in 1989 marked a change of emphasis in his climbing. It also marked the beginning of Buoux's long slide out of fashion. In 1991, Marc Le Menestrel bolted a new line to the left of La Plage and called the project *Chantier* – 'construction site'. Sixteen moves long, Marc later abandoned it as too difficult and Ben himself had a go, completing a majority of the moves. (The story he made moulds of some of the holds so he could practise the sequence at home is true.) But the gulf between the handful of 8cs at Buoux and this futuristic project was too great to bridge. Now known as *Bombé Bleu*, at the time of writing the route still awaits a first ascent, despite attention from Chris Sharma, Fred Rouhling and the Basque climber Iker Pou, and it's likely to be 9b. (It also has the curious distinction of being an unclimbed project with its own Wikipedia page.[1])

In 1989, Buoux had the largest collection of hard routes in the world, but, as Ben explains, 'you couldn't find 9a or 9a+s.' The world's best rock climbers gradually moved elsewhere – Céüse, Margalef, Siurana and Oliana – and rock climbing itself morphed, with the highest sport grades tending to appear on routes much longer than *Hubble* or *Action Directe*, which tested stamina as much as raw power. Those looking for fiercely

1 http://fr.wikipedia.org/wiki/Le_Bombé_bleu

technical sequences went bouldering instead. 'It's easier to find 9b routes thirty metres long than it is to find a Hubble 9b,' Ben says. 'They don't have to be quite so technically hard. Even now the grading system doesn't quite catch the two kinds of route.'

In that sense, Raven Tor was the perfect place to find his next target. British climbers, let alone foreign ones, can be mercilessly disparaging about this crucible of sport climbing. 'It's understandable,' Ben says. 'It's not Buoux or one of the big Spanish crags. But it's on our doorstep.' Because of this proximity to Sheffield, with its cellars and Campus boards and fierce competition, and the angle and nature of the rock, it offered Ben a very specific kind of challenge – short, powerful routes that were often in reality extended boulder problems. You couldn't just get fitter to handle Raven Tor's finest; you had to get strong. (Edwin Hubble, the famous cosmologist after whom the telescope is named, was an outstanding athlete in his youth. The name was Rob Moon's idea.)

As the lines quickly accreted through the 1980s, sketched in like a web, a mythology grew around the 'Snore'. Many of the key figures from British sport climbing climbed significant routes here: Fawcett's elegant *Prow*, and what Ben claims as the best route there, *Body Machine*. Jerry Moffatt's *Revelations*, Andy Pollitt's *Chimes of Freedom* (reclimbed in 1990 by Ben after it lost a large and crucial block), Martin Atkinson's *Mecca: the Midlife Crisis*, *Hubble* and, later on, Steve McClure's *Mutation* – each of these routes is a powerful human story involving months and sometimes years of dedication. After doing laps on the hardest routes, after the umpteenth repeat of the *Powerband*, it's understandable if familiarity bred a level of contempt. 'I mean, if you were coming from abroad,' Ben says, and shrugs. (The negativity British climbers showed their own crags baffled Jibé Tribout: 'I'm a little surprised by the British attitude to their own country. Often when they come to France they say: "we don't have good cliffs, climbing in Britain is not good." But each time I come here I find very good cliffs and very good climbs.' So there you go.)

In trying to explain how it can be that climbers at Raven Tor were doing routes bordering 9a almost a quarter of a century ago, when someone as prodigiously talented as Adam Ondra is only now solid at 9b and threatening more, some climbing journalists have tried to argue that climbers of that period specialised much more, focusing on hard redpoints on routes that suited them, rather than travelling to other areas to try different kinds of routes, or winning World Cups.

It's a spurious suggestion that the evidence doesn't support, but at times, Ben would wish his life were that simple. 'If only it were possible to live on an island, alone with your boulders and your 9a route,' he wrote after doing *Hubble*. 'Beavering away, pushing yourself harder all the time. But I know this is not possible.' The athletic and aesthetic simplicity of a ferociously hard piece of climbing contained a paradox. 'I find the competitive instinct in me both good and bad. I know that without it I wouldn't have realised *Hubble*, but I know also that I haven't found that stillness inside and quietness of mind with my continued lack of success in competition.' It's hard to imagine Jerry Moffatt expressing a similar sentiment.

Knowing which way to turn was an existential problem for Ben. What kind of climber was he? It was the same as asking what kind of person he was, because his identity was so enmeshed with the sport. 'Ever since I first set foot on rock at the tender age of seven years, climbing has been the most important thing in my life,' he wrote. 'In fact I would go so far as to say it is my reason for living and as long as I am able to climb I hope I will. It is from climbing I draw my inspiration for life. It is my direction, ever onwards; the striving always to go one better than before; the challenge both physical and mental; searching for that little bit more power, stamina and mental control.'

In a way, his dilemma captured the paradox within climbing itself. What is it – a sport or an art? Is it simply a struggle to be better than the rest? To create something that lasts? Is it enough to express oneself – in the way a dancer or musician might? Or is it a combination of all three of these? In the summer of 1990 at Raven Tor in Derbyshire such questions were preoccupying not just Ben but Jerry as well. *Hubble* was very much public property – an obvious gap to the right of Moffatt's *Revelations* that Andy Pollitt had bolted and, when it proved too hard, offered up to anyone who fancied a go. Two years before Ben had looked at this problem and thought it impossible. There were, he thought, no holds. A year later, and after his success on *Agincourt* and *Maginot Line*, he saw the route differently. It turned out there were holds, he just had to restructure his idea of what holds could be.

He was also restructuring himself, thanks in part to the influence of Wolfgang Güllich's Campus board reaching out across the globe. He built his own wooden board in the cellar of his new house on Buttermere Road, essentially doing boulder problems without footholds. Jerry Moffatt, who had trained on the original, built a wooden training wall in the basement of his new house in the winter of 1989. Ben was often down there too, usually with a whole gang of honed locals: Mark Pretty, Mark Leach and Andy Pollitt. Ben even had a Campus board in his back garden. It was like strapping on extra rockets of power and lighting the blue touch paper. (The craze for this extreme form of home schooling reached its apotheosis with Malcolm Smith's replica of *Hubble*, screwed to a wooden board in his bedroom. After spending a winter on this, he could do the crux of *Hubble* statically, hanging off the undercuts to chalk up while being photographed.)

All this extra power had an almost immediate impact on what could be done. In 1989 Jerry set to work on a project at Lower Pen Trwyn that he'd spotted a couple of years before. Only a motorbike accident, which left him with multiple fractures, prevented him from completing the route that year. When he finally did complete it, in May 1990, he graded it 8c, the first route at that level in Britain, and now widely judged to be 8c+. *Liquid Ambar* was an extraordinary step up, as well as being an outstanding route in its own right, the best, Jerry claimed, of his career. That success

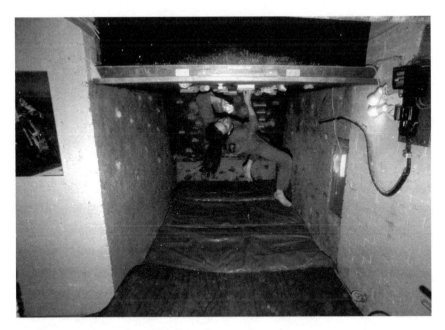

Training in Jerry's cellar. **Photo:** Jerry Moffatt.

must have affected his decision whether or not to continue working on *Hubble* or go instead to a major competition in France. The following year, after quitting the competition circuit, Ben's success on *Hubble* was still on Jerry's mind:

'There was too much travelling all the time. I wanted to climb for myself again. Competitions were good in the beginning when I wasn't good at them but then I found the formula for preparation and won. You have to work and train so hard though and even if you win it's been forgotten a couple of months later. I was working on *Hubble* last year with Ben Moon and with two weeks to go I had to make the decision whether to carry on or prepare myself for this huge competition. I went to France and Ben did *Hubble*.'

'It was a bit like that,' Ben says. 'We were trying it together – it was an open project. He has said that he didn't do it because he had to make that decision. I think it was more a calculated thing that he wasn't sure he could do *Hubble* – maybe not do it and get beaten to it and still miss out on a competition. He did put quite a lot of effort into *Hubble* afterwards as well and didn't do it. He got close. Jerry was an amazing climber and definitely the best in the world at some point. His mental attitude was just brilliant. But he wasn't as naturally powerful and that's what *Hubble* is all about. It was more suited to me than it was to Jerry. What's definitely true is that people don't remember who won competitions, although Jerry's win in Leeds is an exception.'

'Do you see yourself as naturally powerful?'

'I think if others were asked what my strengths were they would say finger strength and power, which I think is genetic.' (This is a perfect example of Ben's understated attitude. Ben's finger strength was, for most of his contemporaries, mind-boggling. One apprentice rock god in the 1990s, struggling on one of Ben's problems, saw him walking by and asked for advice. 'Have you tried pulling harder?' Ben suggested.)

Realising the potential of this immense natural power was the key to success on *Hubble*. After *Agincourt* and a winter's training, the possibility of climbing it became real, but it was still a monstrous undertaking. 'After four days of effort,' Ben wrote, 'out of the seven hand moves which made up the route all but two remained to be done. At this time the route felt so hard that I was unable to imagine how strong a climber would be when he linked all the moves together in a redpoint. I didn't know when it would be climbed but I knew it would be.'

The route got wet that autumn, seeping with moisture, and wasn't dry again until the end of May 1990. 'On my first day I did the two remaining moves and I could now see myself climbing the route but was unsure as to when. By the end of the year, if I trained hard perhaps? Four days later and things had suddenly come together at a phenomenal rate and now begged the question – next day?' It was actually three days later, on 14 June, the day after he turned twenty-four, that *Hubble* was completed. 'It left me wondering where my hard route had disappeared to. I was mystified.'

Thursday 14 June 1990, the first ascent of *Hubble*. 'Did Whore!' **Photo:** Ben Moon Collection.

Ben's response to this immense achievement was complicated. Compared to how he would celebrate completing longstanding bouldering projects later in his career, his reaction was oddly muted. Having knocked off the world's hardest route in the morning, he spent the afternoon training. 'I really did celebrate when I did the sit-down start to *Voyager*. Maybe that was to do with getting older, and success being less certain. When I did *Hubble* it felt inevitable. I knew I was going to do it. I was confident of success.'

Equally, he felt that he was approaching his limit and wasn't sure what to do next, as he wrote at the time: 'One week before I had told a friend that I wouldn't want to try a harder route, that this was my absolute limit; now I had achieved that absolute limit. Grades seem meaningless to me now. Are you any the wiser if I say that it is 8c+ or the hardest thing I have ever done? For what is hard for one person is easy for another. I know that *Hubble* is what I'm best at and of its type is the hardest in the world. I have worked long and hard at gaining the things I need for this type of route.'

It would take years to gain some kind of perspective on what Ben had achieved that day in June 1990. The route was obviously hard and immensely powerful but in 1990 there was no real context in which to frame it. Then there was the vexed question of its grade. It's indisputably the first route of its grade but what grade exactly? The balance of opinion now, taken in the context of modern grading, suggests *Hubble* was not the first 8c+ after all but the first 9a. It's had many suitors, but few have succeeded in repeating it. Malcolm Smith was the first in 1992, but since then it has had a handful of claimed ascents and one of those is doubtful. Steve McClure, whose 9a *Mutation* capped his series of desperately hard new routes at Raven Tor, is one of those who managed a repeat: 'When I was young and super-psyched, and way before I even imagined I'd climb hard stuff, this was the big thing, the hardest route in the world. *Hubble* was the word on everybody's lips. It was the ultimate benchmark. It then gained a reputation over the years; it never became easier, almost harder in its reputation. Second, it's a big deal for me as it's totally against my strengths. I'm rubbish at bouldering and I'm relatively weak and use technique to get up stuff. *Hubble* can't be tricked!'

On the subject of its grade, Steve has been more circumspect: 'It is given 8c+ but the grade doesn't really matter. It could be 9a+, it could be 8b+; it's totally irrelevant. It's the name that matters.' Steve has suggested the crux at a bouldering grade: Font 8B, which, put through the grading currency converter, comes out at 9a. It's also worth adding that people who could cruise 8b+ couldn't do a move on *Hubble*. Perhaps the view of *Hubble* as a boulder problem with a rope, or a micro-route, has coloured attitudes. The current fashion is for sport routes that get longer and longer, like Chris Sharma's 9b *Jumbo Love*, all 250 feet of it, or Adam Ondra's 9b/+ routes at Flatanger in Norway, which are 180 feet long. So where does a route that's essentially seven moves long with some 7c+ above it fit into that scheme of things? 'It is a boulder problem,' Ben says. 'If it had a flat landing you could probably pad it out.' On the other hand, you can't, so you have to wear a harness and tie in.

The fact the route's name still means something and that today's best climbers still want to try it is arguably more significant than whether *Hubble* really was the world's first 9a. Perhaps that's why McClure suggested the grade is not so important; the sequence speaks for itself. When you start digging away at those routes widely regarded as being the first in the world at a particular grade, there are always several other routes that are contenders. Grades tend to arrive like buses – all at once, and from a group, not an individual. Then there are the exigencies of the media and sponsors. The public more readily understand a number and a hierarchy, and so that's what they're given. Top climbers are often more thoughtful, recognising the actual climbing, assessing who did it – their body type and strengths. Wolfgang Güllich hesitated to give *Action Directe* a French grade – he actually rated it XI on the UIAA scale – so the journalist Tilmann Hepp did it for him: 8c+/9a? That question mark was a tantalising invitation for the public to use the higher notation, which they soon did – and a legend was born. By then, tragically, Wolfgang was dead, although many of the world's best do now regard *Action Directe* as a benchmark at the grade. These days, outdoor tourism businesses in the Frankenjura boast that the region has the world's first 9a.

Ben is adamant that *Hubble* is of the same standard as *Action Directe*, having climbed all the moves on Wolfgang's route although thwarted from a redpoint after injuring a finger on it. At least one of those who have been on both agrees with him. By 2014, Adam Ondra, who has climbed over one hundred 9as, and 9a on sight, had tried the route three times, and has described it as the hardest route and boulder problem in the world when it was done. 'It is not the most inspiring line, it seems more like a boulder problem with a rope and easier top-out, but one must admit that it is of revolutionary difficulty for its time and I believe that it isn't by any means easier than *Action Directe*, the world's first 9a established a year later.' On his first attempt, in 2010 after the World Cup in Sheffield, Ondra, feeling jaded after competing, couldn't match the underclings, a move where Scottish climber Malcolm Smith had managed to chalk up while Heinz Zak photographed him. 'A year later, early one morning on the last day of my England trip, I tried hard and could indeed feel a significant difference thanks to some time spent on the Campus board, but despite being close I failed. Strong Britons!' On Ondra's third attempt, again after a hard day and little sleep, he fell three times from the final move. 'Ben Moon was ahead of his time by a huge margin!'

There's no equivalent to a stopwatch or tape measure in climbing, and it takes time to reach consensus, especially at a new level of difficulty. Deep down, Ben believes he was capable of climbing 9a and it nags at him that his achievements might be underestimated thanks to a grading system that is subjective, certainly at that level. When Fred Rouhling claimed to have done the 9b *Akira* in 1995, Ben wrote an article sharply critical of the readiness of some climbers to claim big numbers without justification. Rouhling's response was to draw a cartoon of Moon, having missed out on the first 9a, lecturing his betters. Ben's reluctance to sell himself, to be cool and objective in his judgements, sometimes worked against him. Now, with the new definitive guidebook judging *Hubble* to be 9a, the scale of his breakthrough will receive its due.[2] 'Steve McClure

2 With *Hubble* now rated 9a, Jerry Moffatt's *Liquid Ambar* is likely now the world's first 8c+.

26 Lower Pen Trwyn, 1991: Ben on Jerry Moffatt's route *Liquid Ambar*. **Photo**: Steve Lewis.

27 *Kleinian Envy*, Dinorwig Quarries, Wales. **Photo:** Steve Lewis.
28–29 Ben bolting and attempting *Sea of Tranquility*. **Photos:** Steve Lewis.

30 Lower Pen Trwyn, 1993: *Sea of Tranquility*. **Photo**: Steve Lewis.
31 Climbing *Big Golden* in Fontainebleau, France, spotted by Jerry Moffatt. **Photo**: Jerry Moffatt.

32–33 Yosemite, 1993: Ben on Jerry Moffatt's *Dominator*, and spotting Ron Kauk on *Dominator*. **Photos:** Kevin Worrall.

34 Kilnsey, 1993: first foray on to the project. **Photo**: Steve Lewis.

35 *Deliverance*, Stanage Edge, Derbyshire. **Photo**: Jerry Moffatt.
36 Christian Griffith cuts Ben's now famous dreadlocks. **Photo**: Steve Lewis.
37–38 *The Thing* and *Superman* at Cressbrook, Derbyshire. **Photos**: Stéphan Denys.

39 Bouldering at Shivling base camp, at Tapovan in the Himalaya. The Bhagirathi peaks can be seen
in the background. **Photo**: Ben Moon Collection.
40 Fontainebleau, 1996: repeating Fred Nicole's *Karma*. **Photo**: Jerry Moffatt.

41 The Kilnsey project. **Photo:** Jez Portman.
42 Joe's Valley, Utah, 2000: the first ascent of *Black Lung*. **Photo:** Jerry Moffatt.

43 *8 Ball*, Gardom's Edge, Derbyshire. **Photo**: Ray Wood.
44 Slipstones, 2004: the first ascent of *Cypher*. **Photo**: Adam Long.

45 Stanage, 2005: Jerry Moffatt's *The Ace*. **Photo**: Ray Wood.
46 *Voyager*. **Photo**: Ben Pritchard.

47 *Voyager.* **Photo**: Ben Pritchard.
48–49 Ben, with his mother Beth, and grandmother Ruth (who passed away shortly before publication).
Photos: Moon Family Collection.

50 On the Cuillin Ridge, Isle of Skye, with Ben Pritchard (left) and Ben Tetler (right). **Photo**: Ben Pritchard.
51 Climbing legends at the 2014 Kalymnos Climbing Festival: (L–R) Patxi Arocena, Gerhard Hörhager, Boone Speed, Jibé Tribout, Yuji Hirayama and Ben. **Photo**: Eddie Gianelloni.
52 Sylvie and Jo. **Photo**: Ben Moon Collection.

took quite a long time to do it and he'd already done quite a few 9as and a 9a+. Adam Ondra has suggested the route is 9a,' Ben says, 'and he does climb 8c+ on sight. From reading what he's said, I take it as 9a, so maybe I really did do the first 9a in the world.'

One thing isn't in doubt; *Hubble* changed things for Ben. He had been an enigmatic figure in the 1980s, understood and appreciated among his peers, but not so much by the climbing public. He cut a striking figure – thanks to those dreadlocks and cheekbones – but his media profile was mostly limited to photos. In the few interviews he'd given, he came across as terse and direct, a contrast to Johnny Dawes, whose quicksilver imagination lit up magazine profiles, or Jerry Moffatt, who revelled in media attention and seemed to overshadow him. After *Hubble*, he was more frequently in the magazines and improved his sponsorship deals. The short article he wrote for *On The Edge* magazine about the route was very different, revealing more of Ben's true nature, an admixture of thoughtfulness, focus, sensitivity and determination – the same qualities that appear in his letters to family and friends. The article ends not in triumphalism but in doubt and a renewed sense of purpose:

'I feel that for me to on-sight 8a+ now would be a greater achievement than the climbing of *Hubble*, 8c+. I have a bitter taste in my mouth and I am aware of my weak points. Is it possible to be the best at all aspects of climbing when what is required of each is so different? "But really, it is time for me to turn away from the hard redpoint, for a living has to be made. I must train my weak points, I must control my head and gain technique." I hear those words echoing back from earlier in the year and once again find myself drawn towards the ultimate physical effort. You know, there are some holds on that bulging wall to the right of *Hubble*, I think … '

It seems incredible now, in an era when Adam Ondra and Chris Sharma can travel the world spending weeks at a time redpointing projects to the great satisfaction of their sponsors, that this might once have been a negative thing to do. But in Ben's era, before the rise of climbing films helped promote that kind of lifestyle, one way for sport climbers – as opposed to trad climbers – to get attention and funding was in the new climbing competition circuit, one of several reasons that Ben was so keen to do well in them. In his 1989 *High* magazine interview, Sean Myles had asked him: 'Why did it take so long to go from 8b+ to 8c?' (In the longer view, it hardly took any time at all, but the 1980s were a special case.) Ben replied: 'A lot of people now concentrate on competitions so they can win money and because it's an easier option because ultimately you don't have to be that strong. So now everyone trains for competitions, which is different to [the fitness] required for hard routes.'

There had been an attempt to include the discipline of redpointing in a competition format, to include the large number of French climbers who were good at it, but watching someone work a route really wasn't that interesting to watch. In a debate about modern climbing ethics for *High* magazine from this period, Jerry Moffatt regretted that this feature of competition climbing was fizzling out: 'It's sad for climbers who are good at redpointing but not very good on sight. Ben excels at redpointing; he's one of the best in the world. He's just incredible. But he can't make a living and he's not getting any recognition.'

In fact, any lack of recognition for sport climbing in Britain and the United States was already beginning to change. Christian Griffith, who by now had started his clothing label Verve and would be an influence on Ben in business as well as climbing, wrote to him: 'The American mags finally realised the existence of *Agincourt* and *Maginot Line*. Good effort. Did I tell you I named a shirt in my line after your route? The *Agincourt* reminded me so much of these old linen shirts we bought in France that I felt obliged to name it after that. I'm going to send one back for you.'

Ultimately, the focus – and many of the top climbers – would swing away from competition climbing and back to all the other various forms of rock climbing, not least bouldering, which was already on its meteoric rise. 'It's true that my on-sight ability was not as good as my redpointing,'

Ben says, 'but that was partly because I didn't focus on it enough. To do hard on-sights you need to practise a lot.' Ben's weak reputation for climbing on sight was about to change. Buoyed by his success on *Hubble*, his self-confidence soared and over the next few months he enjoyed a blur of success in several kinds of climbing on two continents.

First, he made a fast repeat of Jerry's *Liquid Ambar* after only five days of effort. 'I was so chuffed with doing it so quickly. I felt more confident. I felt like I was climbing well, training hard, climbing a lot at Cressbrook and getting strong with a lot of endurance.' Ben was full of praise at the time for the quality of *Liquid Ambar*. Neil Foster, reporting *Hubble* and *Liquid Ambar* in the same issue of *High* magazine, wrote: 'Moffatt's route appeared infinitely finer, a fact born out by Moon's enthusiastic pronouncement of the pitch as one of the best routes in the world.'

'I would never put *Hubble* in that category,' Ben says now. 'I think it got one star in the Peak guidebook, and that's probably about right. It doesn't have a line and it finishes in the middle of nowhere. Maybe I'm being too harsh. The moves are really good and it's not an eliminate.' *Liquid Ambar* would have to wait a long time for a third ascent. Exposed to the tide, the time you can spend on the route is limited each day, making Ben's success early on the fifth day even more impressive. It also takes time to dry, and then can get too hot. Even so, plenty of climbers performing well at Raven Tor could make little impression. Pete Robins finally succeeded on the third ascent after twenty days of effort in 2009, almost two decades after Jerry and Ben.

Even more striking was Ben's sudden burst of form on the competition circuit. At the end of July he achieved his best result since his debut in 1986 at the second round of the UIAA's new World Cup circuit. Route-setters at Madonna di Campiglio in the Italian Dolomites had been short of time, with the resulting routes having very hard cruxes while otherwise being not so tough. Competitors could progress easily before getting stopped by one fierce move and would then jump to touch as high a point as possible in order to qualify for later rounds. ('A slap-fest' is how American climber Jim Karn described it. Lots of early competitions were 'slap-fests', until they changed the rules.) Ben was the only competitor in his semi-final to climb the crux and reach the top of his route, and he performed almost as well in the final. It looked like he would get his first significant win until a young and rather tall Frenchman called François Legrand had a go. François, who hadn't even made the French team that year and qualified in the open event, would become the most successful competition climber in the sport's history, winning five World Cups, including that of 1990, and three World Championships. And even then, he struggled to get past Ben's highpoint.

Madonna would be the highlight of Ben's competition climbing career, and he finished fifth in the rankings of that year's World Cup series, a few points behind Jerry. Asked in 1991 why he hadn't mastered competitions, his frustration was obvious: 'I don't know. Fucking hell, I don't know. I just don't know. I haven't got the head for it. I don't like saying that because it seems really negative, but you have to be realistic about these things.' Even now his failure still rankles with him: 'I came very close. I had a few second places. Maybe I wasn't in the right physical shape. I certainly wasn't one hundred per cent focused on them. Jerry was fully committed and I wasn't. I preferred climbing on rock than indoors. All that travelling back and forth, stuck in isolation when you could be outside.'

'Jerry used a self-help book, Lanny Bassham's *With Winning in Mind*, to change his attitude towards competition. Did you know about that?'

'Yeah, I tried all that. I had pieces of paper stuck to the walls with positive messages on them. Didn't work.'

Whatever blockage Ben suffered in competitions, it wasn't lack of ability to climb on sight. In early 1991, Ben was just back from a long trip to Colorado where he climbed an old Christian Griffith project left of Eldorado Canyon's *Psycho* at 8b+. (He called the route *Persuasion*, 'after the Jane Austen novel. My mum suggested it.') In the spring, he headed to North Wales with Mark Pretty and Sean Myles, to explore the Dinorwig quarries. Something about the precision that slate demands of a climber inspired him. In Vivian Quarry, he on-sighted *Manic Strain* and *Kleinian Envy* at 8a and 8a+ respectively; climbing 8a+ on sight was, in the early 1990s, as good as it got. He also made a fast repeat of *The Untouchables*, a Johnny Dawes 8a.

Soon afterwards, he wrote an article for *High* magazine in the form of a letter to an unnamed American friend that sums up what had been one of the richest periods of his climbing life. He carries off this epistolary approach very neatly, leaving nothing out, creating well-drawn pictures of where he's been but keeping the tone easy and confessional, much as he did in his real letters. The article was published as he wrote it, without any kind of introduction, and consequently some readers might have been a little baffled by its contents. Knowing the context, essentially what he had been up to since climbing *Hubble*, it reveals a great deal about Ben's character, motivation and sensibility in his own words. (Further context is added in square brackets.)

'Have you done *Hollow's Way* yet? No? Did you get *Over Yourself*? Good name that one. Has Skip been trying *Hollow's* at all? You must let me know what's happening. [*Hollow's Way* is a classic Font 7C boulder problem at Flagstaff in Colorado.]

'*Hollow's Way* was probably the best thing I did whilst over there. A lot of people might find that surprising perhaps, but it's such a classic problem – most of them are at Flagstaff. It was just so exciting, adventurous in a way. What with not knowing how the moves went, or whether it had been repeated. It felt kind of like doing a first ascent. The boulder was a little dirty and lichenous and the rock a bit brittle. Sounds shit doesn't it? But it wasn't, it was amazing. There I was, alone in this pine forest, looking at this dirty overhanging wall with a flake that petered out a couple of feet below the top. It's quite a nasty landing as well, because your whole body's twisting round itself as you dyno for that flat hold at the top, and there's that tree stump below. And then the feeling I had when I held the flat hold and made the final few moves – God it was exciting not knowing how they would be, and all the time thinking of the old tree stump below. Then I was on top.

'A couple of easier, but still classic, problems later I was finished. Sitting on the top of this boulder in the half-light with the sky turning a deeper shade of blue with every moment; the air crisp, clear and still and Boulder stretching out below me and in the distance the lights of Denver, and to my right the massive rock slabs of the Flatirons. There I was nibbling on a PowerBar and drawing on a pipe, alone. [When he read this, Jack Moon wrote to Ben with grandfatherly advice: 'I see a reference to a contemplative pipe. Very nice if you can keep it under control, but bad for training if you can't!' Jack clearly had an Tilman-esque image of a 1930s *tobacco* pipe in mind. The frequently peddled rumour that Ben used drugs to enhance his performance is wholly wrong.]

'When I first arrived in Boulder I had just planned for my month's trip to be a bouldering one. I would still love to do it. [Climbing *Persuasion* had got in the way.] Buy an open-topped Mustang and just cruise off with a load of friends and go bouldering all over the show. Take a photographer too and get a stack of good photos. Oh well, one day ...³

'Don't know what it is about bouldering, but it's just got it, hasn't it? Guess the freedom has got something to do with it. I really enjoyed that day we had with Christian and Chris at Horsetooth Reservoir. Particularly the Eliminator and Mental Block boulders. There they were, for real, with the painted white arrows and all. Again that was something special, what with having read all about them and the people who climbed, got me really excited.

---

3 Ben was undoubtedly inspired in his dreams of an American road trip by the recent experiences of Sean Myles, who sent Ben a postcard back from the States: 'Frozen yoghurt is rad. The women actually talk to you. Petrol may as well be free. Motorcycles are virtually half price. Radar detectors are legal. If you can climb E6 you are a God. I think I'm dreaming ... '

'Gill, now there's a boulderer. I had had my doubts about how hard he had been bouldering. He was a legend, made out to be a god in that *Master of Rock* book. I think I might have been a bit embarrassed if someone had written that about me. Still he was doing some hard stuff, no doubt about that now. That *Central Eliminator* had me completely stumped. All you had was that sharp little finger hold for your right hand and a poor smear for your left foot. Then you had to crank like a bastard and lay one on for that jug way up there. I wasn't doing that that day. Then there was *Left Eliminator*. Remember that classic photo of the man himself in *Master of Rock*? Just locked off and reaching for the top. My imagination went wild when I saw that photo. Had visions of this tiny finger hold and a shit left foothold and the top being miles away. Ha! The reality was a bit different. The finger-hold was more like a jug, did it first try.

'Then there was that other absolute classic, *The Pinch* on Mental Block. Everyone has seen that photo of John Long in *Games Climbers Play*, dynoing off this broad pinch. Well, there it was for real and I was psyched. So much for the dyno, did the thing static. Hey, but what's this? A rounded, gnarly mantle with a bad landing, good job you were spotting me, because I was off. Not too good at mantles, me. I think you just have to go for it, throw yourself into it, because I did it three times on the trot after I fell off and it didn't feel too bad. [Jack Moon was intrigued by the terminology modern climbers use: 'The modern climbing jargon is totally strange to me. I don't know what a dyno is, or what redpointing or on-sighting are. Or what do you do when you have to crank. But I'm very glad you all use soft footwear. The No.14 Tricouni was a super nail, but death to the rock, which was simply ground away.']

'I am climbing better now than ever before. Bouldering better, on-sighting better and redpointing better. My head's in good shape with the right attitude: determined, positive and, most important of all, motivated. Also my body is in good shape, I feel fitter and stronger than before and aware of my movements. Okay, so I should be climbing better than before but it doesn't always work out like that. I think you just have to keep at it. And often when you're working hard and don't seem to be making progress, you just have to stick with it. I reckon hard work pays off in the end, if not immediately. You just mustn't get downhearted.

'I've been training hard at one particular place, and now have the place completely wired. [This was Cressbrook, in Derbyshire, dubbed Crag X because of access problems.] Including *The Thing*, which is English 7c. Guess it means it just isn't that hard – very technical though. It's taken me a long time to get that move sussed. Trying the move over and over again and each time trying to feel exactly what my body is doing, but trying to feel without trying – do you know what I mean? In the end there was just one little trick, but I ain't going to tell you what it is.

'Done some serious traversing there as well, which I think benefited me loads. It's power stamina I think I want. I always had *Liquid Ambar* in mind when I was doing that. I really wanted to make a quick ascent of that route. First try, fifth day in the end. Don't know how quick that is because I have nothing with which to compare it. I think it's respectable though. I can see someone doing that in two days soon. That would be something else. [Ben would not have believed a third ascent would take nineteen years.] Amazing route, has to be one of the best in the world, top ten at least. You don't mind failing on it if you feel you're climbing at your best. It's that good.

'I've also been climbing more on slate. You know, that funny grey-coloured rock piled up in massive heaps around Llanberis. Johnny always told me I should go there and I never did, said I didn't have time. What an idiot I was. You can be sure I'll take you there when you come over. In fact, I did my best on sight there. A route called *Kleinian Envy* done by Andy Pollitt. Felt really good on it. The last hard move is this powerful dyno off a poor right-hand layaway and being slate there's just this micro edge for your right foot. I remember in the flash of a second looking at the slot

I was aiming for and thinking: 'I've got you.' Then I shot upwards and outward and there it was beneath my fingers, my body tensed in position. I really enjoyed it.

'Anyway, I guess that's about it. I've been taking it quite easy really. I've got a project left of *Liquid Ambar* to finish but it's not that hard, about 8b+ I reckon. [This would become *Sea of Tranquility* in 1993, rated 8c by Ben at the time and now graded 8c+.] Apart from that I really need to find a hard project and soon too. I'm getting the shakes. Stay in touch.'

If Ben wanted a hard project, then, to paraphrase Captain Willard in *Apocalypse Now*, for his sins, they gave him one.

Video stills from *One Summer*, showing Ben training in The School Room. **Photos**: Ben Moon Collection.

WORK IN PROGRESS

'You ask me what I was wearing? Just a pair of old plus fours and a jacket and an old hat – in winter a balaclava. All very amateur. I had a cape in my rucksack with a spare pullover, water bottle and chocolate and raisins.'

Jack Moon, now an old man and in failing health, took great pleasure in following his grandson's career and the link it gave him to his own climbing. He was rooting for him, perhaps with a touch of envy at his grandson's freedom. He could be defensive of him, too. In 1986, he had written to Rob with a cutting from *The Guardian* about Johnny Dawes' new route *The Indian Face* on Cloggy, which hailed Johnny as the best climber in Britain: 'An E9 sounds a bit nasty, but why no mention of Ben?' For his part, Ben would prompt Jack for memories, out of historical curiosity and affection for his grandfather.

'Thinking about the old days I remember some highlights,' Jack wrote to Ben in 1991. 'I had a super fortnight in June 1934 in Skye when Jeremy was on the way. It was so hot my feet got burnt through my gym shoes. Your modern footwear was not around. Such things, together with pitons and carabiners were unknown. I saw a Brocken Spectre, and had a view, from above – which is unusual – of a golden eagle when I was on top of the peak at the end of the Cuillin Range. It really was golden, but didn't stop. I recall with pleasure coming down the Great Stone Chute on Sgurr Alasdair, dropping 1,200 feet in minutes.'

Jack's handwriting was a little ragged by then, but the freshness of his memories is rather moving. These were his halcyon days, recollected if not exactly in tranquillity then in the quiet after the storm. Tired from the effort, he would put down a letter to Ben, and carry on the next day. 'If only I could use a pen I could write lots more, but *anno domini* seems to be all pervasive. A slow but inevitable *descensus averno*.'

Ben was now in that stage of life Jack was recalling in his letters, taking the tide at the flood. His successes, beginning at Buoux in 1989 but especially since *Hubble*, had filled him with confidence. 'I was climbing well, I had a Peugeot 205 GTI, I was starting to make a little bit of money – and I had a girlfriend.'

The latter development must have caused some gossip among his friends; Johnny Dawes had described Ben and Jerry in 1988 as 'shy and pathetically single'. In his 1989 *High* magazine interview, Sean Myles had teased Ben about his private life:

'You've been a full-time climber for quite a few years now?'

'Six.'

'Has that restricted your social life at all?'

'What are you getting at?'

'Well, it's a peculiar sort of life. Quite dedicated. Monastic.'

'Yes, I like that. Climbing is a monastic way of life.'

His relationship with Sarah began in March 1990. She was a literature graduate, emotionally aware and artistic, with no immediate interest in rock climbing but a love for wild landscapes. She connected with the side of Ben's character that took trouble to ask how his friends and family were in letters – the side that loved reading. Postcards home to Beth or to his siblings often had a message in Sarah's rounder cursive hand. From Italy, just before his great result at Madonna, he wrote to Rob: 'Tomorrow the competition starts. I feel good once again! Yesterday I went swimming, and the day before and I will today no doubt. The weather is really cool but the water is nice.'

'This is festival week,' Sarah wrote to Rob from San Sebastian. 'Amazing fireworks and a riot which excited Ben.' (For his part, Ben was looking forward to discussing the recent London Poll Tax riots with his brother.) In Barcelona, just before Christmas 1990, Sarah and Ben are fresh from the Picasso museum, 'drinking strong sweet black coffee. People are yelling and kissing each other. There are some outrageous buildings and narrow streets with really tall houses leaning in and crazy traffic in between.'

Despite the romance, the relationship didn't deflect Ben's focus on climbing. Sarah gave him a desk diary at the end of 1991: 'Dear Ben, wishing you an inspiring, challenging and prosperous year. It's all ahead of you!' Ben kept the diary and others like it for the next few years, not to record his thoughts and feelings, at least not often, but to maintain a record of his training and his physical condition. Professional athletes routinely keep training diaries, and if they don't their coaches do, but such things were largely unknown in climbing until this point. Ben's diaries offer a detailed account over several years of the ebb and flow of a full-time climbing career. As the months flick past, the scale of Ben's dedication becomes clear, along with the rhythms of the training calendar as he builds towards redpoint attempts. They show him at times feeling unmotivated, weak and uncertain, and at others strong and confident. He would grade each training day easy, medium or hard, and then tot up the numbers of each he had managed each year. He would be careful to take rest days, sometimes several, although would often spend these running or cycling in order to work on his cardio-vascular fitness.

On 7 July 1994, for example, he takes amino acid supplements in the morning and then heads to Crag X. He had taken to doing a sequence of boulder problems without rests and timing himself, taking a specified rest and then doing them again. Today, he climbs up and down a 7A+ problem called *Jericho Road* and immediately sets off across and back along the 7C traverse line, *Moffatrocity*, then up and down *Jericho* again, before falling off his second go at *Moffatrocity*. 'Very good,' he records.

'2.45.' He then rests for half an hour and does this again. 'Fell going down *Jericho* second time. Good, nearly made it. Time 2.28.' This time he rests for only fifteen minutes. 'Fell going up *Jericho* second time. Time 2.00.' Another fifteen minutes. 'Fell on *Moffatrocity*. Time 1.22. Very good training this, best session yet.'

And after all that, he heads for the weights room.

Ben was constantly experimenting with new ways to train, new treatments for injuries and new approaches to nutrition, hunting the right balance between power and endurance, keeping his motivation and focus burning brightly. Analysing these innovations, particularly those to do with injury and nutrition, with the benefit of hindsight, he often comments: 'I'm not sure they made any difference.' What made a difference was hard work over a sustained period of time. Occasionally he berates himself for a lack of application. In early February 1995 he's complaining about feeling tired: 'Have been very unprofessional these past few weeks and will get all I deserve. Will pay heavily for two hard nights – Friday and Saturday.' His weight, he records with an exclamation mark, falls to 62.5kg or 138lb. Yet clubbing kept him sane, offering a release from the intensity and focus of his training week.

Sometimes he wonders if the training hasn't taken over the climbing. In Volx a few days after regretting his two nights out on the trot, he tells his diary: 'Feel like I am climbing absolutely terribly. Really inefficient. Feel great deal of pressure and want to start enjoying my climbing again. Need to do some routes, just some ticking. There is no doubt I'm very strong and reasonably fit. I've just forgotten how to climb and what it is like to do a route. Had some long talks with Zippy and [Scottish climber] Spider [McKenzie], and came to some good conclusions and new decisions. I am still able to look at my climbing objectively and know what it is I need to do.'

Norman Mailer, in his account of the 1975 fight between Muhammad Ali and George Foreman in what was then Zaïre, writes about the immense psychological weight of constant training: 'In heavy training fighters live in dimensions of boredom others do not begin to contemplate.' As Mailer points out, that is where boxers need to be. The boredom engenders a kind of restless anger that ultimately finds an outlet in violence: 'Boredom creates a detestation for losing.'

Mailer likens the training boxer to a man serving a long jail sentence, how the scale of his boredom, its unrelenting pressure, will tip him towards despair. 'Sooner or later the fighter recognises that something in his psyche is paying too much for the training. Boredom is not only deadening his personality but killing his soul.'

Then again, as Ali himself acknowledged, the depth of your ability – its heft – and the confidence to succeed can only be built through training. 'The fight is won or lost far away from witnesses – behind the lines, in the gym, and out there on the road, long before I dance under those lights.' Except that for climbers it's different. What you struggle against in climbing is failure itself. No one is waiting for you in the ring, there's just ambition and the passing years – and the endless, endless training.

'It's why I packed in route climbing,' Ben says. 'Training is time consuming.'

'Tedious?'

'It's not tedious. Well, maybe it is. But you need a lot of time – hours and hours each day. Your lifestyle changes because of it. It's not very glamorous, is it? You've got to knuckle down. These routes, they're like an iceberg with all its mass under the surface that no one ever sees.'

'In some of the entries in your diary you seem quite depressed.'

'I don't think I was. It's not the right word. I don't get depressed. I might feel a little down, but that's it. Mostly I get annoyed that I'm not doing well, that things aren't going my way. I'd get fed up at not being motivated. I'd be doing the same problems again and again. It's a thin line between caring deeply and it becoming pathological. It's a pretty lonely thing. It's not easy. Not that many people could do it for a long time.'

'Was it easier training with other people?'

'It's fun with people, but I would tend more to do it by myself. Unless you have the perfect training partner it's easier to do that side of things on your own.'

Ben and Jerry were often in each other's company in the early 1990s. These two were so committed and so strong, that several of those in their orbit span off in new directions, incapable, for lack of means or motivation, to do what seemed necessary to be at the leading edge of sport climbing. But although they trained together, they were motivated differently. Crag X became a favourite training location, a brutal curl of polished limestone where Ben and Jerry added powerful problems. *Superman*, at Font 8A+, was Jerry's best-known contribution. As the rock ran out, Crag X acolytes began eliminating holds to create new and harder problems. Ben even managed to eliminate holds on *Superman*, and was delighted. Jerry, on the other hand, was furious, not because Ben superseded his problem, but because Ben seemed content with doing desperate things in training and not converting this progress into something more eye-catching somewhere less humdrum. Yet for Ben, the realisation of something previously unimaginable was success in itself.

His training pattern changed somewhat in 1993 when The School Room opened. This training facility was the brainchild of a group of Sheffield climbers led by Gavin Ellis. With the help of Ben and Allen Williams, Gav designed and then built, with Ben Tye and Andy Coish, a wooden bouldering wall in an old classroom at the disused Heeley Bank School, which Sheffield City Council had turned into a community centre, much of it rented by artists as studio space. Unlike cellars, The School had grand views across the city, but the scale of everything was somewhat surreal: tall ceilings and hooks near the floor for little coats, imposing stone doorways and tiny sinks and toilets.

Gav and his team built four boards at different angles: fifteen, thirty, forty and fifty degrees. Ben's favourite wasn't the steepest; he preferred the

Ben training in The School. **Photo:** Stéphan Denys.

thirty-degree board, which had smaller holds and more accurately reflected the angle of hard limestone climbing. Screwed to these boards were
hundreds of small wooden holds, each one numbered. Combinations of
numbered holds were named and entered into a sort of guidebook. There
was, for instance, a problem called *Polemic in a G String*. Its sequence
read: 'LH A2, RH A5, LH A11, RH B6.' Like the DNA of the perfect
climber, this was coding for the perfect move. Not a move, *the* move, the
perfect integration between a problem and a climber's body shape,
strength and proprioception, a matrix of grace and power hidden in
apparently random combinations of numbers and letters – in its way,
a form of abstract art. Next to this code the word 'SHAFT' appeared,
written in capitals: 'Same hand and footholds.' It didn't matter where the
move was found: Crag X, The School, or Boulder. It only mattered that
it existed. If there has ever been a Zen school of climbing, this was it.

Pinned to the dusty wall was a list of the hardest problems at The School, formulated by Andy Bowie who also wrote the guidebook: 'This list contains some of the hardest problems in the world, ever, and ticking anything in the top thirty is a noteworthy achievement (anything in the top ten is just sick and a level of respect gained unlike anything the world has ever seen.) The list is perfect and is not dependent on height or anything. If you don't agree with it, you're wrong, and you've obviously got a big weakness in your climbing. In fact you're shit, so leave me alone. I have spent a lot of time compiling this list, and disagreeing is fruitless as (like all climbers) I know best.'

The School must have looked baffling to earlier generations; what would Don Whillans have said of it? Or Ben's grandfather Jack? But the banter, the friendship and rivalry didn't seem that different from any other form of climbing, nor the instant, arcane culture that grew up around it. In his training diary, early in 1995, Ben writes: 'Mr Blobby/Woodology. 10 min. Mr Blobby/Woodology. 12 min. Mr Blobby/Woodology. Fell first hard move.' It's like a mantra from a forgotten religion. Nothing captures the mood and intensity of Ben's training pattern than *One Summer*, the film he made with Ben Pritchard, not quite the first bouldering movie ever made, but pretty close. The School features heavily, as do other regular stops on their training circuit: Crag X, Stoney and Stanage. The film closes with footage of Ben from The School working his relentless way up and down a campus board. In a surreal juxtaposition, the voice of Jonathan Agnew is in the background, updating cricket scores. *One Summer* is not a perfect film, but this is one of its several perfect moments.

In early 1992, he was still in pre-School, training at Broomgrove Road and in his own and other climbers' cellars, especially Jerry's. As so often, he was concerned about a possible lack of variety in his training: 'Warmed up at Froggatt. Too windy and pretty horrible. Went back to Jerry's and trained on my own for two hours. Mega session again. Don't know if I am stronger than ever before, or whether I have it all wired. Maybe a bit of both. Must be benefitting me. Did everything. Everything! Nearly first try as well. Pissed the slopers and the roof footless. Worked new problems and did some of them.' Finding everything easy was sounding an alarm bell. 'Am I strong?' he asked his diary a few days later. 'Very little variety in my training at the moment. Usually: warm-up at Stoney. Do everything first try. Train at Jerry's. Do everything first try, more or less. Must get more variety.'

On the other hand, he wrote regularly about how strong he felt, stronger than he ever had in his career. When in 1991 an interviewer asked him about 'working a hard route like *Agincourt*,' Ben stopped him: 'It isn't that hard a route any longer. It might be for some people, but it's not for me. I did it two years ago and a year after, when I went back to it, I did it straight away. It's not state of the art.' Recognising he could move things on, and feeling stronger and fitter than he ever had before, Ben had good reason to feel optimistic. In late February he was in Fontainebleau, and back again in mid March. (Written in Sarah's handwriting for 17 March, are the words: 'Our anniversary.' Ben wrote a few lines below: 'Love Fontainebleau.')

By the start of April, Ben was in Buoux, climbing routes like *La Rose*, until recently state of the art, almost effortlessly: 'Walked it,' he wrote. 'Easiest ever. Unbelievable. Tired from drive as well.' He repeated *Maginot Line* too, his second 8c creation from 1989. He had judged *Agincourt* to be more sustained, but the crux of *Maginot Line*, a dyno for a three-finger pocket, was excruciating and easy to get wrong. He had written after the first ascent: 'For some reason, perhaps pressure, I was unable to commit myself to the redpoint attempt. I could not just turn the motivation on. It was so frustrating, if an 8c was unable to motivate me hadn't I better just pack up my bags and go home? How much of a supreme performance is in the head, I shudder to think.'

The right state of mind to achieve the best possible performance was a constant preoccupation throughout this period. 'Picture yourself doing the moves,' he told himself. 'Picture yourself doing the route and don't let thought interfere with your body. There is no thought involved in our finest moments and this is how it should be. There is no time for thought, just unconscious action.'

Hitting the three-finger pocket on a steep wall at the end of a dynamic stretch was like catching a ball while diving. 'I think here more than else-where it is really important to let yourself go and not make a conscious attempt to get the pocket, not to think: 'I have to take it right.' Your body will have learnt the location of the hold and will know the movement and direction required. Thinking about it will only interfere with what the body knows it has to do.' Controlling the swing following this dyno was almost as demanding, and then another hard move, where Alex Duboc had repeatedly fallen on his redpoint attempts. 'I couldn't say why it was, but there was something in me wanting to give up, something pulling me backwards, but only for a second and then I was committed, I had made the slap rightwards, held the sloping hold, shared and was on the rest.'

Patrick Edlinger, Ben wrote, had since repeated *Maginot Line*, and found a new sequence involving 'a crafty heel and toe jam which eliminates all the swing, the feet staying on the rock. Oh well, never mind. I always used to say that technique is no substitute for power, but it looks like it was here. During his days working the route he felt it to be 8b+, now he has done it he says 8c. Not having been on the route since this new method was found, it is difficult for me to comment, although unfortunately I think it is to be hard 8b+ now.' Back in Volx after three years, he used Patrick's sequence and confirmed his suspicion. He did it again, the old way – and for a third time, but statically. 'I felt unbelievably strong,' he wrote in his diary. 'Absolutely amazing – strongest ever by far. I mean it felt *casual.*'

And in that frame of mind, he left for the Frankenjura, and Wolfgang Güllich's new super-route, *Action Directe*. This line of grimly overhanging one-finger pockets on the Waldkopf in the Krottenseer Forst was soon widely regarded as the hardest route in the world, the first to be regarded as 9a, although Wolfgang himself had simply awarded it the German grade of XI. Ben, like Jerry and most other leading British climbers, believed that experiencing routes all over the world on different kinds of rock was an essential requirement in testing your limits. 'I never thought I'd have a particularly hard time doing this,' he says, 'but an exception was *Action Directe*. It was a route that absolutely suited Wolfgang – short, very steep, very dynamic but there are no tricks. It's a bit like a Campus board.' The photographs of Wolfgang training on a campus board for the route on the tips of one finger were published in magazines around the world, adding to its lustre. 'In terms of raw power he was incredible,' Ben says. 'Looking back now on his career, what he did was amazing.'

Ben hadn't climbed much in the Frankenjura and the specific challenges of the Waldkopf were new to him. On the first day he managed all bar the first individual moves at the start of a campaign that would extend through most of April, although actual climbing days were limited by the extremely cold weather. There was snow on the ground, and keeping his fingers warm was difficult. 'After five days, I was right up there, three days working it and two days redpointing.' His diary entry for 16 April reveals how the weather was undermining his progress. 'Very cold, miserable day. Warmed up at Krottenseer, felt very undecided about trying *Action Directe*. Shouldn't have. Too cold. Briefly worked it, felt very good. Redpointing to move 10. Felt best ever. Really strong but couldn't feel fingers – too, too cold. Fell on move 10 again. Very nearly had it. Definitely if the weather was better.'

Ben had got within a few moves of the top after only a few days on the route and there's little doubt he would have had the second ascent with better conditions. 'It's a very specific kind of climbing. It's on pockets but they're different from Buoux-style pockets. They're semi-crimpy and you put immense pressure on your tendons.' The cold didn't help either. 'There was snow on the ground and it was impossible to stay warm for a redpoint.' On 22 April, after a fortnight in Germany, the inevitable happened – he tore a tendon in his fingers. 'I was really devastated, partly because I hurt my fingers pretty badly. I could never climb hard on pockets after that.'

At least it had given him an understanding of how hard Wolfgang was climbing, and how *Action Directe* compared to *Hubble*. 'I always said that it was about the same grade as *Hubble*, right from the word go. Zippy and I were staying at Wolfgang's house. He was away working as a stuntman on the movie *Cliffhanger*. His wife Annette was there, and I remember chatting with Wolfgang on the phone one day and telling him what an amazing route it was. He said he was looking forward to coming over to try *Hubble*.' Wolfgang was serious about visiting the Peak District that autumn, but he never got the chance. Returning from an early morning radio interview that August, his car veered off the road and he was killed. 'Dying like that after all the crazy stuff he did in Patagonia and the Karakoram just seems incredible. He was such a nice guy, so humble. I can't believe that both he and Kurt [Albert] are gone.'

About a month after injuring his finger, Ben was climbing again, but it took months before he fully recovered his strength. A week before Wolfgang died he climbed *Hubble* again. 'I think I'm as strong as I was at the beginning of the year,' he wrote on 21 August. A few days later, Malcolm Smith got the second ascent, prompting a flurry of exclamation marks in Ben's diary. He was impressed. Ben spent that day training at Jerry's house with Zippy and Mark Leach. 'Bloody knackered at the end. Good session. Must do something new now.' First he had some unfinished business in the Frankenjura. By late September he was back in Germany for another try at *Action Directe*. 'Physically I feel good but left hand third finger terrible,' he wrote in his diary. 'Abandon all hope for **this year**.' But he never went back and his fingers never truly recovered.

Repeating other people's masterpieces was – and, as Adam Ondra shows, still is –essential for a leading rock climber. 'You've got to do other people's routes,' Ben says. 'You've got to understand how you're climbing. I want to be the best I possibly can, so it was natural to go on other people's routes.' Ben also needed a new challenge, a way to take his own climbing on from the success of *Hubble* – the next step into the future. What else was the point of so much effort? But if he needed to refocus himself in the same way he had after breaking his wrist in 1988, he still found himself distracted by his fascination with competitions.

In the spring of 1993 he was at several events in Europe and was frustrated in all of them, baffled and angry at his inability to replicate his immense power and ability on rock in a competitive setting on plastic. Things started well in his first event of the year at Frankfurt. He qualified easily enough, got off route in the semi-finals but still managed to qualify, and then messed up his final. 'Dog shit. Where was my stamina? My fight?! Too relaxed? Got pumped and fell off. Should I be more aggressive? Am I not determined? Look to Innsbruck. My win. Must beat those bastards. Must fight. Have you wanted it enough?'

When he got to Innsbruck in late April, things just got worse. 'Climbed absolutely appallingly. Worst for a great many years. Not sure why. Bad day? Bad warm-up? Bad attitude? Who knows? Forget about it.' The day after the competition he comfortably on-sighted a 7c+ at the Wasserfalls, well within his ability except, inexplicably, in competitions. He then spent a happy and successful fortnight climbing hard in Germany and Austria, before failing to get past the semi-finals at a World Cup in Zurich. At the end of May in Toulon, he didn't even get past the first round. His brief diary entry summed it up: 'Disaster.'

Yet between Zurich and Toulon, he climbed one of his best, most difficult and least known hard routes, the project he had mentioned in his article in *High* three years earlier. *Sea of Tranquility* takes a line through the steepest rock at Lower Pen Trwyn, just left of *Liquid Ambar* and at the same grade. The crux is desperately hard, in the words of Pete Robins, the only man to have repeated the climb, 'a hideously powerful

AUGUST 1993

Saturday
14

Tried project on lower Pen Trwyn. Warmed up on E3 + E5. Greasy conditions. Climbed up + down start of project. Worked top crack. Wet + little gripping ended up pumped. Worked hard bit. Had two redpoint attempts + fell both times on hard move. No way in these conditions.

med

drove to Wales.

1993 AUGUST

11th after Pentecost Sunday
15

Much better conditions. Warmed up on E5 and up + down, start of project. Felt good. Worked top crack once + hard part. Had four redpoint attempts and did it on last go. 1st try ¾ hour, 2nd try 1 hour, 3rd try 1 hour, 4th try climbing well although maybe I should have done it on 1st go. Conditions did vary though and last go was best. Greased off on maybe 1 of the goes. Great feeling and managed to keep my head.

med

drove to

Sunday 15 August 1993, the first ascent of *Sea of Tranquility*. **Photo: Ben Moon Collection.**

sequence on disappointing slopers,' and would be rated Font 8A were it climbed off the ground. Robins got the second ascent in 2010, more than seventeen years after Ben, and praised the route's quality. Ben had repeated *Liquid Ambar*, also rated at 8c+, the year after Jerry's first ascent and in doing so helped build the route's reputation. Perhaps because *Sea of Tranquility* wasn't an advance on *Hubble* – being graded 8c at the time – the climbing world just shrugged and moved on. Without someone to confirm its quality, one of Britain's most difficult, and best, sport routes slipped into obscurity.

It's now almost twenty-five years since Wolfgang climbed *Action Directe*, and Ben climbed routes like *Hubble* and *Sea of Tranquility*, and yet they are still seen as impressive achievements by today's generation. Not so Ben's on-sighting ability, which has been totally eclipsed. Climbers competing today are required to on-sight an 8c or 8c+ to complete the final route at a World Cup. If absolute technical grades have moved on only a fraction since the early 1990s, the on-sighting ability of today's climbers is far in advance of what was being done then. In 2013 German climber Alex Megos on-sighted the 9a *Estado Critico* at Siurana in Spain. The pool of climbers able to on-sight if not 9a then 8b and up is also much larger than it was twenty years ago. It puts into perspective both how the sport has and hasn't moved on and how extraordinary Ben's redpointing ability was.

Finding the right project was his biggest challenge. He had a few in mind, the route at Pen Trwyn, which he worked on in March that year and finished in May. There was another in Dovedale, and he top-roped the bold line at Burbage South then known as the Yoghurt Arête, which became Neil Bentley's *Equilibrium*. (This was in late summer, 'which probably explains why I found it so hard.') As a top-rope problem, it had a Font 7C+ crux; as a lead it was a much wilder beast and not what he wanted. Ben also knew of another project, an old aid line at Kilnsey, climbed in the 1960s, like several of the routes going free at that time, by John Sumner. Mark Leach had looked at this, and replaced a couple of the bolts, but soon abandoned the project to Ben. 'He always used to joke I stole his project.'

Mark was famous for the level of effort he showed in realising his ambitions. 'He got incredibly committed to routes,' Ben says. 'He has an incredible work ethic.' *Cry Freedom* at Malham, perhaps Mark's most famous route, took forty-six days. *The Screaming Dream*, a micro-route at Froggatt Edge, took over fifty. Ben repeated both these routes, doing *Screaming Dream* second go. ('Sometimes I thought he could get a bit blinkered in finding a sequence and then sticking to it, even if it wasn't the right one.') Overcoming *Cry Freedom* – Ben's was the third ascent – took longer. 'At the time, I thought I was making a meal of it, but there's still very few who have done it and everyone who has says it's hard.'

The first mention in his diary of his Kilnsey project was 13 June 1993 and it would figure in his life as a constant presence for the next three years. Ben had not done a great deal at Kilnsey, certainly nothing harder than 8a, and wonders now whether his lack of experience of the crag made him underestimate the problems he'd face with his new project, especially with seepage. For much of those three years, the route was often wet. First he had to get the line in shape. He spent a day drilling bolts and cleaning off loose flakes, walking an ethical tightrope in having a route that was solid and clean but unmolested. 'There's always going to be loose rock. You can be selective about what you take off and what you don't. If you come across a hold that's loose and it's key to the route, you've got to glue it. I never pulled anything off, stuck some glue on it and put it back. But if something were a bit wobbly, I'd put glue in the crack to keep it there. I know what's right and wrong. I've never taken a hammer to a hold. I've never picked something off the ground and stuck it on. I never drilled a hold. I might have chosen what I left on and glued something I needed. If you've got a really spiky hold that's ripping your fingers then I'd take an Emery cloth to it. The chances are you're making the hold smaller when you do that. You want a route to stay as it was so everyone tries the same thing.'

At first, he was worried that he'd wasted his time. 'Certainly sustained,' he wrote in his diary in late June. 'But not at a very high level – shit! Certainly not as hard as I wanted. Maybe 8c? Did some quite big links. Good route though.' In early July, he was starting to revise his opinion. He linked a lot of easier moves together 'up to the blank bit', and rated this section at 8b+. 'Difficult to say how hard it's going to be. Could just scrape into 8c+ bracket, I hope. Felt pretty good climbing it and excellent conditions.' A few days later, and the route was looking harder.

'Worked crux section for the first time. Did all the moves, all four of them, but not in a link. Very technical and powerful, very hard. I worked the very top section too, which also felt hard. A week later he was back but discovered the lower section was wet. He managed to link together the dry upper section and was still thinking that he'd soon have the route finished. But he spent August training and travelling to Bulgaria for another abortive competition.

Ben didn't get back to Kilnsey until early September. Even though he managed his best effort so far at linking together moves, the scale of what he was attempting was beginning to dawn on him. 'This was my best day on the route, [but am] powering and pumping out and haven't even reached the crux. Route seems very, very hard – 9a.'

He had found what he was looking for, and it would cost him everything.

Sunday 14th after Pentecost
5

Restday - cricket

Week 36 Monday
6

was suposed to be trying my route at Kilnsey. But I felt far too depressed and actually hating climbing. Steve persuaded me to try it. Bolt to Bolted it and it didn't feel very hard. Then about 2 hours later when I was cold + everything, tryed one redpoint. Fell off usual place I min rest went to top. Need to get my head sorted out and do it on my next day. Still sore from cricket. Hate life.

Mad

September 1993, head games on the Kilnsey project. **Photo:** Ben Moon Collection.

UNFINISHED
MASTERPIECE

Three days after his most positive attempt yet, Ben was back in Yorkshire, but his impetus and focus were crumbling. 'Was supposed to be trying my route at Kilnsey,' he wrote in his diary. 'but I felt far too depressed and eventually hating climbing. Steve [Lewis] persuaded me to try it. I bolt to bolted it, and it didn't feel very hard. Then about two hours later when I was cold [I] tried one redpoint. Fell off usual place. One minute rest, [then I] went to the top. Need to get my head sorted out and do it on my next day. Hate life.'

Where had the optimism gone? What had changed in those three days? Ben was experiencing the first real personal crisis of his life. 'Sarah had been at the Edinburgh Festival with her best friend and when she came back, she sat down in the living room and said, "I'm leaving you." It was the first time I'd experienced what that was like. I was devastated.' Splitting up from Sarah prompted Ben to re-evaluate what he was doing with his life. 'I began questioning climbing. I was having constant conversations with Sean, blaming climbing for the relationship not working. I remember soon after we split, driving out to Crag X with Sean for a bouldering session. Obviously in those circumstances you don't want to do anything. I hated climbing, and was blaming it, and Sean was saying: "No, that's not the reason you split up." There was also the rejection, which I guess nobody likes. I suppose I was feeling what everyone does when they're dumped by their first love. It's not easy. In retrospect, I can see that I was too focused on my climbing and put it first too often.'

To escape the sense of loss in his life, Ben threw himself even deeper into climbing, despite his anger at it. The day after his redpoint attempt at Kilnsey, he was climbing *Nectar* at Stanage. 'A soulful day,' he wrote in his diary. He was training intensively but couldn't obliterate Sarah's absence from his mind. A day later, he is complaining about a friend's cellar board being too easy, and that he can't get pumped at the Foundry. 'Up, down, up, down. Very depressing.' That same afternoon he goes for a six-mile run, seeking oblivion in exercise. 'Cannot just mope around,' he writes next day, after spending it at Crag X. At the end of October he flew to Germany to prepare for the next round of the World Cup in Nuremberg, where he finished sixth, his best result of the year. But instead of committing to the final round at Laval in France, he travelled to Yosemite to spend the weeks before Christmas bouldering, mostly on his own.

After a few weeks in the Californian sunshine, Ben was beginning to adjust to life and wrote a long letter to his sister Georgina, working as a teacher in Greece, about his state of mind and how climbing and the things he loves about life are restoring his balance. In contrast to his matter-of-fact diary entries and his terse interview style, he is much more open, revelling in the natural beauty around him and taking pleasure in a really productive few weeks of climbing. It's 8.30 a.m. He's sitting in the cafeteria in Yosemite, drinking coffee, waiting for Sean Myles and his girlfriend to join him for breakfast:

'It is very cold here early in the mornings and in the evenings when the sun goes down at about 5 p.m. Being outside most of the time can be physically and mentally very tiring. My routine is get up, go to the cafe, go climbing, go to Sean and Jo's for supper, go to bed. It's a simple life-style that is proving most of the time to be very satisfying. For the first two weeks I was camping with some English friends but they have now left and I am camping alone. I was a little apprehensive about how this would be but – cross fingers – it's actually been quite enjoyable and so far I have had just the right amount of company and solitude. I have a good book to read and have just bought myself a Sony Walkman, so now I have music as well. Climbing has been (as I knew it would) a great support to me over the past months along with a few dear friends.

'The climbing here is probably some of the best in the world and I am climbing exceptionally well, even if I say it myself. This is not to say that life has been easy the whole time – it hasn't. But just when things seem to be getting on top of me, I am rewarded with an ascent of a special climb and the appearance of life changes for me, for the better. I had a list of things I wanted to do before I came here and yesterday I finally ticked off the last and hardest climb on that list. This means I can more or less relax although I probably won't since there is so much more to do here. Sean is also trying to persuade me to go away from here for a week, perhaps down south towards Mexico, so who knows.

'Beyond the road are just miles and miles of wilderness. Huge granite monoliths rise out of the pine trees on the valley floor for thousands of feet and in the distance are snow-topped peaks, waterfalls, huge waterfalls, and rivers abound. Since being here I have seen much wildlife, coyotes, bobcats, racoons and wild deer. There are also bears. Not only is the climbing excellent but also the walking. The other day I went on an eight-mile hike alone up to the top of a **huge** waterfall and then on to a highpoint called Yosemite Point. I stayed on top for as long as possible and have rarely felt such complete satisfaction. I just lay on the yellow granite boulders in the late afternoon sun and gazed over the distant peaks of the High Sierra. The sky was an amazing blue and the air crystal clear. I watched a nearly full moon rise in the east, the sun going down in the west and all my worries and trouble dissolve into nothing. I remember reading something by Turgenev about the effect nature has on man. He says something about the fact that nature, mountains, streams and so forth are complete or whole, kind of perfect I suppose and this inspires a similar mood in the onlooker. It was something like that and I know how I felt then and won't ever forget it. I didn't want to leave but had to.

'What else do I want to tell you? Sometimes I worry about what I am writing and who I am writing it to. People are so reserved – including me – and I do not want to be. Surely it's bad to bottle things up but I wonder what people including you will think of what I write. I am probably worrying unnecessarily. I hope the teaching is going well and we do see you at Christmas.'

Ben skates over his climbing news, not wanting to bore his sister, but when he sat down to write to her he must have been buzzing with satisfaction. On the end of the list of problems he'd wanted to climb at Yosemite was Jerry Moffatt's incredibly hard *Dominator* at Camp 4. Yosemite, not surprisingly, is globally famous for its big granite walls, but even before bouldering became popular, it was one of the best places for this form of climbing as well and with their background in powerful Peak District bouldering, several British climbers had excelled there. Sean Myles had climbed an outstanding hard problem that spring, dubbed *Cindy* after the barmaid who demanded to see his ID before serving him beer. Jerry's *Dominator*, also climbed earlier that year, was, at around Font 8B, perhaps the hardest boulder problem in the United States. Its three moves cost Jerry weeks of effort. Not only did he starve himself to be as light as possible, figuring that at only three moves he didn't need any stamina, he even dried his chalk in a microwave to give himself an extra edge.

When Ben arrived in mid November, he recorded his thoughts on being introduced to Yosemite's most famous problems. 'Was shown all the classics: *Blue Suede Shoes, Cocaine Corner* etc.' Near to *Cocaine Corner*, on the Wine Boulder, he was shown another of Jerry's problems from that spring – *Stick It*, easier than *Dominator* at 8A, but still horrendously difficult. 'Seemed hard,' Ben told his diary, 'but suddenly did it and not too bad. Probably took eight or nine tries. Tried *Dominator* crux about three times. Seemed hard. Then I did *Midnight Lightning* second try.'

Ben settled in for a long campaign to repeat *Dominator*. Five days after first seeing the problem, he was still absorbing its challenge: 'Tried *Dominator* for about probably two hours. Couldn't do crux move, very hard, hard to tell how close I am. We will see.' Ill health kept him away for a few days, and when he recovered he found himself getting frustrated 'and losing skin' as Yosemite's granite took its toll on his fingers. 'You take what's there and it isn't much. Right hand big rounded layaway; left hand good edge; right foot small smear; left foot good edge. Then it's jump! Left hand catches a small flat edge, feet immediately swing off and a fraction of a second later you're back on the ground again.'

Like Jerry, Ben had learned to be immensely disciplined in taking rest days before attempting a hard problem, so he waited until he was fully recovered and tried again on 1 December: 'Worked *Dominator* move for an hour and a half,' he wrote in his diary. 'Twice very nearly did it. Don't know what the secret is. Felt strong on it. Best ever. 45 mins coffee break and a PowerBar and did it third or fourth try! Mega feeling, very happy.' A few months after the first ascent, Ben had got the second. There wouldn't be a third until 2002 – nine years later.

'I spent six hours on the one move,' he wrote afterwards, 'before finally realising it and yet I am still unaware of what I had done differently to all my previous attempts. Six hours over three days over three weeks. What really happened during this period?' The move, Ben suggested, was more about power than technique, but he questioned what that meant. 'What is technique? What does it encompass? Even powerful footless moves require technique. Perhaps with these types of moves we are not aware of the effect of the slightest change in body position, swing, speed of movement and co-ordination. Technique is not only about how you move your body but how you work your muscles.'

As always, the state of mind in which the body can perform to its absolute limit was foremost in Ben's mind. '"The consciousness of self is the greatest hindrance to the proper execution of all physical activity" wrote Bruce Lee.

"It is about letting go and allowing the body to adapt to the demands placed up on it. This is attained through concentration. The concentrated mind is a still mind and a still mind is a mind that can know things as they are." I wanted to know things as they are; I wanted to know it all. Perhaps it's right that I'm unaware of what, when I finally held that swing, I had done differently. I do know that it felt good, really good. To find myself after all that time on new territory, to have moved on that little bit further to a position in space that I had never been to before. My feet swung out as usual but then they swung back in and seconds later I was on top.'

He started 1994 in a renewed state of determined effort, drawing up a training plan to fill in time before another trip to the States. The pattern of his climbing life is exposed in his training diary; he gradually raises the level of what he's doing day to day, focusing on what he judges to be his current weakness. 'Don't think I'm as strong as two years ago,' he writes in early February from Fontainebleau, but climbs a new 8A. Later in the month he manages a problem at The School that he rates at 8B. Establishing such a high base level allowed him to raise his standard slightly at just the right moment. That month he also started work with Ben Pritchard on what would be the first British bouldering video – *One Summer.* Pritchard was climbing and training regularly with Ben, and to a high standard, and understood intimately the scale of Ben's ability and effort. There are long, almost meditative sequences that capture his intensity and commitment as perhaps nothing else has since. Ben had a great deal of creative input into the final version, filmed on videotape in the age before digital cameras, and consequently a beast to edit. He cared deeply about the project, writing to his mother from Buoux at the end of the year that he was worried about its reception: 'I hope you don't find it too boring. I keep getting nervous about whether it will sell and I so hope it isn't a complete flop.'

In March he flew to Denver, where his old friend Christian Griffith finally persuaded him that his dreadlocks were holding him back, and cut them off.

'I think he wanted to be the one who did it,' Ben says. (He kept them, but later lost track of them moving house.) Then – lightheaded – he headed west with Jerry and his girlfriend Emma, and Kurt Albert, for a road trip, crossing Colorado and Utah to Nevada where, Ben wrote to Rob, he had 'nearly done everything. Did you visit Las Vegas? It's an incredible place, totally mad.' In a postcard to Beth, he wrote: 'Sitting here in Red Rocks, Nevada, and allowing the pancakes I ate for breakfast to digest. Weather is perfect, clear skies and 70° heat. In a couple of days we are off to Joshua Tree, California for more climbing. Yesterday Sean and his girlfriend Jo arrived here so now there are six of us. It's funny how we have all met up here. Can't help wishing there was one other person here but I must be strong. Really am having a great time and I do so like travelling especially when the company is good.'

When Ben got back to Britain, he and Sarah tried again, another twist on the emotional rollercoaster he'd been riding. He returned to his training regime, equipping himself for another summer on the Kilnsey project, now dubbed *Fusion* – a good name for a futuristic power project. In May he climbed a longstanding Font 8B project at Stoney Middleton – *Pinch II*. This was hardly the sort of success to grace the pages of the international climbing press, but Ben was delighted. 'Very strong. Tried it fifteen or twenty times and finally did it. So, so pleased. Another goal achieved.' After that success, he headed to Kilnsey for the first time that year to test his progress: 'Felt stronger than last year but power endurance nowhere near as good.'

Ben was still struggling to find a balance between his climbing ambitions and his personal life. At the start of June he headed to north-west Scotland with Sarah and climbed Stac Pollaidh: 'I remembered afresh what it's like to reach a summit. I think there is still the spirit of a mountaineer in my soul.' On a postcard from Ardmair, she added a note about Ben leaping to the summit 'like a grasshopper'. Yet the relationship wasn't enough to deflect him; Ben was still intensely driven to succeed at one thing in particular,

Video stills from *One Summer*, the first ascent of *Pinch II* at Stoney. **Photos**: Ben Moon Collection.

to move the standard of sport climbing forward a notch. On 13 June, the day he turned twenty-eight, Sarah wrote in his training diary: 'This is your birthday. Take time to reflect on your life and loves, your aspirations and achievements. Then drop a tab and forget everything but the present moment.' Underneath, Ben had written: 'Trained at school with Jerry and Stuart.'

Back at Kilnsey, he fretted about his physical readiness: 'Compared to last year I am way down on endurance. Need to do more traversing at Cressbrook and Raven Tor, more campus.' His emotional state was also in turmoil. By early July Ben was in Italy for a photoshoot and his relationship with Sarah was over for good. 'Climbing has been my life for a very long time, and it must have been very hard to be with someone who is that driven and focused. A lot of people go through life and never discover something that motivates them like that.' He had been wholly torn about what to do, recognising that he was 'too focused on my climbing' but not yet ready to put it aside when his ambition still burned so brightly. 'The situation definitely impacted on the Kilnsey project. Emotionally I was a bit fucked up. I was down. I remember being at Kilnsey with Chris Plant at the redpointing stage, and bursting into tears. Chris put his arm around me. I wasn't in a good mental state.'

He reassessed his fitness in early July, and decided not to go near the route for a fortnight, preferring instead to train for endurance. By mid July he judged himself 'strong', always an ominous sign in Ben's diary. 'Much more powerful than last year. Just need to convert it to more endurance.' By the start of August he was back on the route and getting close. 'Should have, could have done it. Bottled it a bit. Very annoyed with self. Totally knackered at end.' Climbing's old guard had routinely dismissed sport climbing as having no psychological pressure to it, but all Ben's hardest achievements in climbing had come with a huge psychological price tag – none bigger than his attempts on *Fusion*.

At least he knew he was on the right track. Fabien Mazeur, a rising star of the French sport-climbing scene ten years younger than Ben, was in Britain that summer. Fabien, tragically killed in a car crash the following year aged only nineteen, had just repeated Jibé Tribout's new hard route *Superplafond*, which built on Ben's 8c *Maginot Line* at Volx. 'Fabien had been doing well in competitions and asked if I minded him trying. He set off and I could sense that he thought he could on-sight it. The first three metres [in a route of fifteen metres] are easy but then he got to the first hard move and was off. It took him forty-five minutes to dog the route to the belay.'

By the end of August, Ben felt he was closer than ever but the route had become a little damp. 'I feel very good. Next day? Just need a few dry days. Could well do it this year.' On 2 September he was 'even closer. Should even more so have done this. Again, felt **very** strong. Feel very good at the moment. Have it very wired and feel super strong. Bottom no longer hard. Should be able to do it next day.'

There would be no next day, not that year. Autumn rains meant the route was wet. 'Don't feel massively disappointed,' Ben wrote in his diary. 'In all, things this year went pretty well. Maybe, probably did, started my power endurance too late. Did more than enough power training, partly due to filming bouldering videos. Two more weeks of dry weather and the route would have been in the bag.' Ten days later, and the focus and intensity of the last few months had dropped away. 'The year is pretty much over for me. Just India. Just?! Then maybe a bit of training, Christmas, training – then France.'

The trip to India, partly inspired by Beth's trek in the Himalaya, had been something he had planned to do with Sarah. He went anyway, and afterwards would regularly cite his experiences as among the best of his life. His plan was to meet friends from Norway he'd got to know in Buoux and then head for the Garhwal and the village of Gangotri. From there, it was a two- or three-day trek, past Gaumukh, the cow's mouth, the glacial cave regarded as the source of the Ganges, to Tapovan, a pasture at 4,400 metres spread with boulders. It would be mid October before they got there, and freezing. To prepare himself for the privations and physical challenge of bouldering in India, he walked up to Derwent Edge to do an E5: 'Really pretty cold today and big walk in. Mustn't complain because India is going to be *very* tough.'

'Am still alive and don't seem to have caught the plague,' Ben told his mother in a postcard, on arriving in Delhi, where his friends were conspicuously absent and there really was an outbreak of plague, which caused the largest mass migration in India since independence in 1947. 'I have to confess that on the plane I was rather wishing it was going to London not Delhi. At times I felt really quite panicky.'

A few days later he was in Gangotri, still somewhat panicked by the demands of life in India. 'Against all odds, we made it here. We have survived the plague, political upheaval in Uttar Pradesh, and these high mountain-passes. You know what it is like here but I can't help telling you. It has surpassed all expectations. Sometimes it feels like heaven on earth.'

From Tapovan he sent her a card with a picture of the Diwan-i-Khas at Delhi's Red Fort on the front. 'Of course, we're not in Delhi but it's all I have up here. Today the man that runs the restaurant, nothing more than a tent, is bailing out, so I can give him some post. It's pretty much the end of the season here and it's only the Babus and the hard-cores [sic] that are left. The weather is pretty good except for the last two days when there's been a howling wind rushing through the meadow. When there is no wind it's warm, nearly hot but at night the temperature must drop to at least -10°C. Haven't done a great deal of climbing mainly due to headaches, which I think are caused by altitude. I certainly feel better and more energetic as each day goes by I have to confess though that now I am here I am more interested in the mountains and just exploring the surroundings. Too much to write about, not enough space.'

As much as he loved the mountains, Ben was not about to become an alpinist. Only days after returning from India, and without the few weeks training he'd promised himself, he was back in the south of France for the first time in over two years. 'I know the place so well that it could have been only last week,' he told Beth. 'It's good to be here though, particularly since the weather in the Peak was so miserable when we left. Here it is predictably hot, too hot in fact for hard climbing but hopefully as the days go by it will cool off. The first week has flown by and I am not climbing very well but I didn't expect to be. I am trying what is generally considered to be the hardest route in France.'

This was *Superplafond*, Jibé Tribout's extension of Ben's own route *Maginot Line*, which Jibé had originally dubbed *La Lune dans le Caniveau* – the moon in the gutter. It linked Ben's route with the top of an 8b called *Terminator* to create an 8c+ and was widely regarded as the hardest route in France, a power-endurance route that suited Ben. Another French climber, François Petit, had also added an 8c+ to Orgon's Canal sector, notorious for its chipped holds, called *Bronx*. 'Moves seem ridiculously easy,' Ben wrote in his diary. But his weeks in India had eaten away at his endurance. On 29 November, he wrote: 'Very unfit. How quickly will it come back? Very good session. Know the route well.' By the time he came home for Christmas, as usual to visit his mother in Kingston, he hadn't done either route: 'Don't feel massively disappointed. Climbed well, really.'

The next few months would prove pivotal in Ben's life, in some ways a high-water mark of what he was capable of doing as a climber, but also a breaking point, as though the last of the motivation that had carried him forward for a dozen years had been dispersed on the wind and lost forever. There were hints of the future in January. Although he felt himself to be the strongest since his last attempt at Kilnsey – 'But how can I be?' – he berated himself for spending too much time clubbing and not enough training. He was being 'unprofessional' and would 'get all I deserve.' When he arrived in Volx, where he railed to Zippy and Spider about his drop in fitness and form, he felt himself to be moving badly, and complained in his diary about a lack of technique. After a week in France, his confidence was dented after failing to climb a 7b+ at Cimai on sight.

'Very depressed. Felt like giving up climbing.' Then he got back on the route and drifted up it, able to rest anywhere, suddenly trusting his footwork and keeping calm. As he knew from experience in competitions, it was often his mind that defeated him. His body was more than capable. If he could only disconnect his anxieties and climb like he didn't care, then it would be easy. In this mood he tried an 8a called *En Un Combat Douteux* on sight – and strolled up it: 'Very comfortably and totally in control. Climbed brilliantly. Totally calm and relaxed.' A few days later at Orgon he redpointed 'pretty comfortably' an 8c, *Macumba Club*, that was very much a stamina climb with some fifty separate moves, and on-sighted a 7c+.

This confident frame of mind proved fragile. Over the next few weeks he made a huge effort to climb *Bronx*, spending eight days on the route, with success apparently within his grasp, before failing for one reason or another. (This was still much faster than Jibé.) By the end of March he'd had enough: 'Orgon again. Bad night's sleep. Woke up in the middle of the night thinking about the route. Can't take much more. Decided to make this day the last on the route. Give it all I have and then leave it. Will cease to enjoy it after today. Read very profound paragraph in *Zen and the Art of Motorcycle Maintenance*: "Mountains should be climbed with as little effort as possible and without desire ... to live only for some future goal is shallow. It's the sides of the mountain that sustain life, not the top. Here's where things grow."'

The next day did not seem propitious. 'Did usual warm up but didn't feel especially strong and conditions [were] not brilliant. Started to rain. Worked route very briefly. Just did the moves once. Concentrating on footholds. Thirty minutes rest – no visualisation but prepared for big battle.' There was no battle. Ben just fired through the moves, focusing not on his hands but his feet, letting his fingers work automatically through the holds, letting his mind wander off where it couldn't get in the way. With *Bronx* in the bag, he almost climbed an 8a+ on sight, getting it second go. He was elated. 'Brilliant day. Hope I can climb like this

Bronx. **Photo**: Ben Moon Collection.

more often. Hope this will prove to be the tip of an iceberg. Can do much harder stuff than this. This is just a foundation to build on. I'm a better climber than I was three weeks ago. Have learnt a lot.'

Two days later, at Volx, he worked through the moves on *Superplafond*, figured out some better sequences, did a few links and pronounced himself ready. 'Conditions brilliant. Did it first try, really easily. Didn't use *Terminator* rest, felt totally relaxed and probably climbing my best ever.' This was a hugely impressive effort; *Superplafond* had been an open project and Jibé had trained specifically to get the power necessary. Even then it took him seven days to redpoint. Ben had now got two 8c+ routes in the bag, and a couple of days later climbed his second 8a on sight – *Roseanne* at Céüse. It was time to go home and start thinking about Kilnsey again – and to train intensively.

On 8 April, he records a bouldering session, some problems at The School, work on the Campus board, circuits, and after all this he writes: 'Can't really do anything hard at the moment due to my finger. Feels pretty bad.' For the rest of April he eased off on the training to protect his injury, and then stepped it up again during May. By the end of the month he was ready to go back to Yorkshire.

At first, he feels he has picked up where he left off the year before, when success was so close. He works out a new sequence on the crux but drops it. He berates himself for a night out that has left him feeling weak. 'Time to get serious. Fingers feel bad again. Must go back to one day on, one off. Also a little ill. Fucking bumbly.' He is most concerned about his 'Action D finger', which had never fully recovered. On eight separate occasions through June he made the long drive north from Sheffield, even warming up at The School before driving to Kilnsey, convinced it was doing him some good. He'd entered the strange, paranoiac world of the sport climber too long on a project, whose desperation to finish is getting in the way of actually finishing. The pressure was intense. By early July he is getting close, doing long links of moves. 'Getting top section very wired. Need to work more on bottom section,' he told his diary on the second of July. A week later there was just one single word: 'Progress!'

After that, there is nothing. The diary is blank until mid September.

All dedicated climbers have to deal with injury. 'It's inevitable,' Ben says. 'It's unavoidable. I did get a lot of finger injuries, every year, or every other year. But they always seemed to get better.' This one could not have been timed worse. For three years Ben had been planning his life around one route, organising his training year to bring his mind and body to a peak just at the right moment. It had been a colossal effort that contributed to the end of his relationship with Sarah. Just when it seemed he might finally succeed, he was injured. Something in his mind said: 'Enough.' He never went back. It wasn't starting a business, or getting married that stopped Ben; it was the intensity of what he was doing. He simply couldn't face it any longer.

'Motivation is everything,' he says. 'You can't train without it. And after three years I didn't have it anymore. Where does motivation come from? It's really fickle and I lost it right there. That's why I didn't do the route. You can't just turn it on. There are little things you do to keep yourself motivated, little goals and so on, but there's only so much you can do. After three years I didn't have it. It was the easier option to pack it in and go bouldering. I hadn't fallen out of love with sport climbing. I just couldn't make the effort any more. It is much more time consuming to do sport climbing at your limit than it is to do bouldering.'

'You could have a life as well?'

'Yes.'

It wasn't so much a decision as a realisation. By mid September he was climbing again, easing his way gently up 7a routes, and then stepping it up to 7b+. At The School he thought he would try some of the easier problems but was shocked to find he couldn't. 'Did the first usual warm-up problems but just too nervous, paranoid, **scared**! Couldn't tell if I felt slight twinges or whether I was imagining them.' His fitness improved, but he still didn't feel confident on small holds, and as Ben put it in his diary: '7b+ isn't very hard, even with no rests. I need to go somewhere new. I want to go bouldering.' It's easy to understand, with the fear of injury plaguing his self-confidence, that Ben couldn't face returning to the intensity of training he'd managed over the last few years, only to get injured again and waste that investment. 'I remember Sean [Myles] wondering if keeping motivation for so long was a good thing.' He told himself that he'd take a year off and come back to it later, but in the meantime life took over. He was done.

'It's a big regret of mine,' Ben says, and the Kilnsey project is a subject he returns to often. It sticks in his memory like a splinter. 'It was the biggest regret of my career. I spent around thirty days on that route. I only spent ten on *Hubble*, eight in reality. I'd done all the moves. There wasn't a sticking point; I'd climbed all of it. I'd gone all the way to the top from just above the crux move. If it had stayed dry in 1994 for a couple more weeks I would probably have done it.'

When Steve McClure climbed the Kilnsey project in 2000 he called it *Northern Lights* and graded it 9a; Adam Ondra repeated Steve's route in 2010, taking seven tries on redpoint. Ben maintains that the line of holds Steve followed differed from the line he was trying. 'At eight metres you go into a shallow scoop, come out of it slightly left and then back right to a pocket and then straight up. Steve went into the scoop, made the hard move left, then kept left for a few more moves, before the sequences rejoined to the belay. At no point could I stop and chalk up, but the way Steve did it he had a point where he could shake out.'

Steve himself admits that his line through this section varied from that which Ben was trying: 'Ben's sequence featured powerful moves on good holds but with absolutely no rest – it didn't suit my style. I took in potentially harder moves, but getting the shake-out made all the difference. It felt like the obvious way to climb the line.'

The Kilnsey project. **Photo**: Steve Lewis.

There's not much to be gained in entertaining the counter-factual for long. Ben knew that his project was a step up from *Hubble*, increasingly regarded as the world's first 9a. Did that make his Kilnsey route 9a+? Perhaps there's a better way to look at it. Many well-known climbers – boulderers, sport climbers or alpinists – talk about pushing boundaries and limits. It's part of the mythology, a useful strapline for sponsors marketing their athletes. The reality is that very few do, but Ben was one of them. He could have spent the years after *Hubble* putting up new routes at a similar level and keeping his face in the magazines, but he chose something harder – and riskier. That it ended in failure is, looking at it from one angle, neither here nor there. He was hunting the future, not resting in the past.

And yet – and yet – from another perspective it's simple: failure hurts. 'I'm not tortured by it,' Ben says. 'The bouldering made up for it. But now I'm back into climbing and feel quite strong, it's in the back of my mind.'

Ben in Joe's Valley, Utah. **Photo:** Ray Wood.

MOON
LANDINGS

In a letter from 1991, Jack Moon told his grandson: 'I shall be very interested to see how your career works out: a few years at the top, and then maybe a climbing school plus a retail shop or shops? Who knows? It is clear that you are not going to be deskbound. At least I hope you aren't. I grew up in the days when it was customary to follow in father's footsteps, as I did, but with hindsight I realise it was his choice and not mine. But in the 1920s and 1930s there were three million unemployed and a safe haven was greatly to be desired.'

For twelve years Ben's focus had been to improve as a climber: training, travelling and thinking about little else. At first, after his finger injury, he concentrated on healing, anxious not to overdo it and set back his recovery. But by December he was starting to feel strong again and began setting himself targets. By March, he could write in his training log: 'Possibly the strongest day at The School ever.' But the years of assiduous record keeping and anxious speculation scribbled in his diary were coming to an end. As his motivation petered out – and he suffered an elbow injury – detailed notes on training were replaced by business meetings and plans for the future.

In early 1996, he had a lot to keep him busy. There was a new film project, directed by Simon Tucker, a friend of Jerry's working at the BBC. Like *One Summer* it's a pure bouldering film, but is otherwise a very different beast.

It opens in a gritty, monochrome Sheffield with Ben, his cropped hair now peroxide blond, somewhat improbably wielding a sledgehammer in an iron foundry to the trance hit 'Schöneberg', before knocking off and climbing into his BMW M3 EVO II. (This was Ben's new pride and joy; the left-hand drive, 2.3-litre, four-cylinder engine produced 217hp, essentially the road version of the car BMW were entering in Group A rallying and touring races.) Where *One Summer* was slow and accumulative, *The Real Thing* is fast-paced and slick, driven on by its techno soundtrack. Ben stops to pick up Jerry, who more or less steals the show, mugging to camera whenever it points at him as the two of them prepare for a trip to Fontainebleau, where Ben repeats Fred Nicole's problem *Karma*. There are speeded up sequences of the two rock stars, aping scenes from The Beatles in *Help!* – two lads who changed the climbing world. Most people usually prefer one to the other of these two cult bouldering films; *The Real Thing* is very much boys on holiday, culminating in a now legendary scene shot in a nightclub: 'Mega night in Paris,' Ben wrote in his diary.

The Real Thing does feel more dated than *One Summer*, unsurprisingly given the music and hairstyles, but there's much to enjoy in it and some poignant moments. Although essentially the Ben and Jerry show, the film features other climbers, including Sean Myles and the late Kurt Albert, who plays his guitar in the obligatory party scene, very much the life and soul of the party. Marc Le Menestrel also appears, his climbing style a smooth contrast to the raw power of the Britons. Marc climbs a classic Font 8A *Le Surplomb de la Mée* and tucked away, almost out of shot, is something that boulderers had lived without until that point – a bouldering mat. In *One Summer* and *The Real Thing*, climbers were landing in the dirt, risking injury, and some horrible falls feature in both films. That was about to change, and it would have big implications for the direction Ben's life would now take.

It took two visits to Fontainebleau to get the necessary sequences for *The Real Thing*, and in between Ben was involved in something wholly different and more significant. The Newbury bypass – in reality a bypass for a bypass – was a nine-mile stretch of dual carriageway planned to relieve congestion in the town and whose planned route drove through an area of outstanding natural beauty and three sites of special scientific interest. Had the public enquiry into the scheme been held a fortnight later, then new environmental impact legislation might have stopped the destruction of some ten thousand trees and the local extinction of a rare species of snail. (On the upside, structures on the bypass won the grand prize in 1999 at the Concrete Society's annual awards.) Protestors, deploying tactics and experience learned at Twyford Down during the construction of the M3, set up a series of camps along the proposed route, digging tunnels and rigging platforms in many of the biggest trees, a practice dubbed 'tree-sitting'.

To remove these protestors, the contractors clearing the site hired a rope-access company, Richard Turner Ltd of Chesterfield, which in turn hired ten local climbers to do the work at £25 an hour, ten hours a day, six days a week – decent wages now, let alone then. However, the prospect of climbers using their skills to help such an environmentally damaging project caused outrage among a climbing community still in touch with its anarchic roots. Climber and writer Jim Perrin told *The Guardian*: 'If we, as a community, do not disown and ostracise these mercenaries and renegades, we are undermining the reason for our own existence and helping accelerate the destruction of places we hold most dear.' The issue was much discussed at a climbing festival in Llandudno held that February, and a number of Sheffield-based climbers decided to go down to Newbury to help the protestors and persuade the climbers working for RTL to quit. Among them were Adam Wainwright and John Redhead, as well as motoring enthusiasts Johnny Dawes, Jerry Moffatt and Ben Moon. Arriving in a super-powered BMW did not endear him to all the protestors but his expertise was welcome.

Some of the long-term protestors, living in fairly squalid conditions, might have looked askance at the fit young man in the Beamer, but it made perfect sense in the context of Ben's life. After all, The Mob, environmental anarchists, had been his favourite band as a teenager; activism genuinely meant something to him, a way to remain connected to the wider world through all the intensity of climbing. The presence of so many climbers certainly helped the protest in its last-ditch resistance. Charles Arthur at *The Independent* reported how one of the RTL workers, Pete Bukowski, had quit after discovering he was trying to evict Chris Plant, a friend from Sheffield. There were also allegations that RTL hadn't followed best practice, allegations Richard Turner firmly refuted as 'sour grapes'. Ben was arrested and escorted from the site: 'The bailiffs would have a hell of a lot trouble getting [the protestors] out of the trees without the rope access guys,' he told *The Independent*. 'And our going down does make a difference. I spent twenty minutes talking to a guy who I know pretty well, persuading him it was wrong.' A photograph of him being lead away by police appeared in the broadsheets. Newbury was, for many of those who were there, a seminal moment in their lives. It brought together many different strata in society; Ben recalls well-dressed elderly ladies bringing cake and tea to the crusties and hippies living in 'benders' high above the ground. The new road brought only limited relief to Newbury's original bypass; there are now plans to upgrade the A34 to a six-lane highway north of the M4.

By April, with filming for *The Real Thing* done and the road protest over, Ben was back in Sheffield and training again. But he continued to be troubled by injury; written in green ink on many days through the spring were the words 'bad elbow'. Worse, the motivation to start over with the kind of intense preparation he'd managed for the last three years was gone. With his thirtieth birthday imminent, he opted to take a year off, and review the situation after a rest. In the past, when he'd felt his enthusiasm flagging, he kept working and waited for it to come back. This time it didn't. In early June he was out on the grit with Steve Lewis and Chris Plant: 'Three hours soloing on Stanage. Want to get back into climbing solo and sort elbow and confidence out. Very, very enjoyable day. Did quite a lot of climbing and a few routes I've wanted to do for a long time. *Wuthering*, again, *The Asp* and *Black Hawk Bastion*. Just taking it slow and steady, working out the moves, going when it feels right. Want to do more of this.'

The most obvious way 'to do more of this' was bouldering. 'People don't always realise how time is a factor on sport routes,' he says. 'In bouldering it's over in a matter of seconds. Routes take a lot more work. Redpointing is way more pressurised than bouldering. Travelling, having a partner, working – these things add to the pressure. Bouldering you can do on your own if necessary. I quite liked climbing on my own. You can be more focused and do exactly what you want to do.'

As a consequence, the pattern of his training life changed dramatically. The circuits at Raven Tor became a thing of the past. 'I hated those problems. That's why I didn't climb there for ten or fifteen years. The bouldering at Raven Tor was more a means to an end. I did a thing there called *Ben's Roof*, figured it out in a few minutes. It's turned into a Raven Tor classic. I even stopped going to Cressbrook. I had a much greater focus on grit.'

Ben was a major figure in the bouldering revolution that consumed the climbing world in the 1990s, not just for what he climbed but for the businesses he started. Britain's leading boulderer of recent years, Dan Varian, described Ben as one of the 'driving forces behind bouldering going from being a niche training activity to a sub-sport in its own right. Before 2000, bouldering was more about training for routes and less about the big clean lines; eliminates and traverses were much more important than they are now. Gradually the onus shifted to the concept of the clean, impossible-looking lines. Ben really cottoned onto this early on and it didn't hurt that he had a set of the strongest fingers in the world at the time and a good eye for a project.'

Yet the truth is that for Ben it wasn't important to find ways to push the limits of bouldering in the same way he had with sport climbing.

After *Hubble* he had been looking for the next step up. That wasn't his motivation now. 'Maybe grades meant more to me when I was younger.'

'Were you happier bouldering than sport climbing?'

'No, I don't think I was. It was just a different kind of phase. Bouldering is in some ways more creative – more aesthetic. You see these beautiful shapes and you just want to climb them. That's why I was so attracted to Fontainebleau. It's magical. The boulders are actually boulders, and it's like they are floating among the trees. The boulders by themselves are beautiful. If you get a pure line on a boulder there you just want to climb it. I also love sandstone, although I can't claim I have a particular preference for types of rock. But the rock quality at Fontainebleau is superb and the quantity of problems is incredible. And the style of climbing – slopey, technical and varied – really appeals to me. The place has got a big history and that appeals to me as well. The only drawback is the weather, which can be unreliable.'

Jim Perrin had written of sport climbing that 'the performer only exists in the absorption within his art, perhaps is reaching the incommunicable.' If that was only partially true of sport climbing, it certainly is of bouldering. Short routines of incredible difficulty on aesthetic boulders in beautiful locations with little danger or narrative lend themselves much more to film or photography than the written word. The explosion of interest in bouldering happened because bouldering allows you to climb hard moves without the same commitment to training or the hassle of redpointing. Like surfing, it seems to bring people back to nature. It spread so far and so quickly thanks to the internet; it really is a climbing medium for the digital age. You can watch Ben climbing *Cypher* at Slipstones in North Yorkshire, find out where the crag is and the best route to drive there, read the opinions of others who have climbed the problem and then share your attempts on Facebook or Twitter. What most of us can't do is fathom the intricacies of its crux, at least the way Ben climbed it, swinging his left leg at exactly the right speed and moment to allow his left hand to slap upwards, his right hand on a poor sloping hold that will only stick for a moment.

'Slipstones was', Ben says, 'one of my favourite spots. It's such a special crag, with its views across the moors. That's one of the great things about bouldering, the places you go.' This from a man dismissed for suggesting he didn't 'climb to be in pretty places'. He would go there on his own, just to soak up its energy, revelling in the immense space while pinned to the sprinkling of little buttresses along its crest. The ten years he spent bouldering seem now a collage of similar intense, beautiful fragments: drifting through the woods at Meschia with the brilliant Italian Mauro Calibani, who knew where to gather chestnuts and would roast them on a stove, fuel for some of the most beautiful problems in the world; flashing the 8A+ *Diaphanous Sea* at Hueco and hearing Dave Graham say: 'You killed that thing!'; sitting on dead leaves at Cresciano, wreathed in cigarette smoke, the mountains white with snow, watching Malcolm Smith powering up *La Proue* on hydraulic arms, his own shoulder tender from a snowboarding injury. Bouldering gave him freedom to travel the world but still do something meaningful as a climber. All the other aspects of climbing he had loved as a child now crowded back in; it was no longer just about performance.

The surge of interest in bouldering opened new markets for information and gear. In the past, no one had bothered keeping a systematic record of who did problems first and where they are. Now guidebooks began appearing dedicated to bouldering and a few of the more enterprising stars began marketing the specialist equipment being developed to meet the needs of this new branch of climbing. Clark Shelk, for example, stuck together his first crash mat with duct tape, got better at it, and started making them for his friends. He made a dozen or so and took them down to the bouldering Mecca of Hueco to sell over the course of a climbing season from the back of his truck; they were gone in a fortnight. Pretty soon, he had orders coming in from around the country and he named his new business Cordless. Rob Gilbert and Dave Bell set up Pusher, another brand that helped to define the bouldering boom that swept across America – and of course the most successful of them all, prAna, began in 1992. In Europe, Mauro Calibani started E9, named after the British climbing grade.

The vibe was more surfing or yoga than climbing, whose brands were more about fabric performance and technical excellence than bouldering's cool admixture of hanging out and bursts of athletic intensity. The culture that grew up around bouldering's sudden popularity – the specialist equipment companies, the surge in digital media – meant this longstanding branch of climbing suddenly felt new, as though it had been invented recently and not way back in the nineteenth century. Ben, with an instinctive feel for fashion, could see an opportunity to reach this constituency. In the early 1990s he had signed a sponsorship deal with Stone Monkey, a rock-climbing clothing brand launched by hardware manufacturers DMM. There had been talk of sales commission and input into the design, but these didn't materialise and Ben was essentially used as a face to sell the brand. He already had the example of his old friend Christian Griffith, who had started Verve a few years before. Now he had the time he needed to set up his own business. 'I knew that the sponsorship wouldn't last much longer, so I had to get on with it while I still had a bit of a name.'

Ben named his company S7, the postcode in Sheffield popular with climbers thanks to its low rent and proximity to the Peak District. Initially, he worked with partners, Mike English who runs the successful Rock City wall in Hull, and Gav Ellis, the energising force behind The School, who was by then working in the rope-access industry. The product range was pretty much everything that Ben used in his climbing life that wasn't already made by established brands: climbing holds, a wooden fingerboard, t-shirts and bouldering mats. Mike and Gav had their own companies to run – Gav now runs his own multi-million-pound access business

– and so Ben was soon left to run this fledgling bouldering brand on his own. Although sales were relatively modest, S7 immediately caught the wave of interest in bouldering and Ben's credibility as one of the world's leading exponents gave his company a real advantage. As the clothing range grew, he inevitably came into conflict with his obligations to Stone Monkey, and that relationship ended.

His life at this stage was full of changes and new directions, as though abandoning sport climbing had let the rest of the world rush back in. At a New Year's Eve party at the end of 1998, Jerry Moffatt introduced him to the woman he would marry. 'He'd been telling me about this incredibly beautiful girl he'd met, how he thought we'd get on, and how her dad had a Porsche.' If Jo's dad shared Ben's passion for motorsport, having raced sidecars in the 1970s, Jo herself shared his passion for travel. In late spring they travelled to California; Ben was asked to appear in a climbing competition at the X-Games in San Francisco and Jo went along. He and Jo spent an idyllic fortnight camping and climbing in the desert, visiting his brother Rob who was living and working in Los Angeles – and crossing the mountains to go bouldering at Bishop.

Pretty soon Ben had the chance to go and live and work in America himself. Within a couple of years of S7's launch, Ben had got offers to buy the brand, but his lack of experience left him wondering what to do next: 'I knew nothing about selling a business. How do you value it? How do you set up a deal like that? Wild Country wanted to buy it at that point, and I remember them offering me £3,000. I remember thinking that didn't sound like a lot of money.' When Pusher came in with an offer to pay off the business loan Ben had used to launch the company, and offered £10,000 on top of that for half the business, he took the deal. 'I was bloody naïve, but it probably worked out for the best. I learned a lot. It all fell apart very quickly but I hadn't invested anything and came back to the UK to start again.'

With the deal came a move to the US to continue working for S7 under Pusher's new owner, Mike Uchitel. 'It was already going wrong when

I got involved,' Ben says. 'He was new to the climbing industry, and we thought he was a business guru because he had loads of money. He spent lots on advertising and on a bouldering competition series, which offered a purse of $20,000 to the winner.' The PCA tour was a big hit, and Mike Call's videos of these ground-breaking bouldering events still feel fresh and exciting fifteen years on. It was clear that interest in bouldering was growing fast, but Mike Uchitel wasn't the first businessman to overestimate the financial potential of climbing. 'What he was doing was unsustainable, and it was hard to get information. I wasn't getting a salary, but Mike would write me a cheque here and there. None of us could work with him. We all tried to gang up on him and force him out but that didn't happen.' With debts piling up, particularly for advertising in climbing magazines around the world, S7's UK distributor pulled the plug. So did stores in America, just as Pusher ramped up production. 'It was a car crash.' Clark Shelk put Pusher and Cordless on to life support and eventually paid off the company's debts, and Ben and Jo flew back to Britain to lick their wounds.

At least Ben's brief business connection with the US gave him the chance to do some world-class bouldering. Before signing away S7, he came out to America to test the waters and ended up climbing with Jerry Moffatt in Utah. The plan was to move on after a few days to Bishop and Yosemite, but Boone Speed, then working with Pusher, and the brand's unofficial photographer, showed them an unclimbed problem on the hard sandstone of Joe's Valley, an area he'd discovered and developed with Mike Call. As far as Ben and Jerry were concerned, that was it. They stayed put and laid siege. The problem was only three moves, focused around sloping finger pockets that required perfect conditions, but it offered, in Ben's words, 'everything that is good about bouldering.' Steven Jeffrey, the local hard man and bouldering Font 8B, had tried this deceptively simple challenge hundreds of times and not done it.

The British photographer Ray Wood had joined them for the trip and watched how the two veterans, now in their mid thirties, fell into a

Cleaning the holds on *Black Lung*, stood on Jerry and Boone's shoulders. **Photo**: Ray Wood.

familiar competitive pattern over the problem. 'Jerry wasn't climbing well but Ben was getting close. With Jerry it was out and out aggression. Ben was the better boulderer, smooth and a bit more powerful. But you never realised with Ben how hard he was fighting, because he doesn't give much away. They weren't overtly supportive of one another. They would have fallings out, but they always stayed mates and put up with each other getting frustrated or losing their temper.' As always they prepared thoroughly, taking two rest days before their final attempt on the eve of their flight home. It was still cold in the desert, which offered perfect friction, but that also meant the threat of snow showers, and although Ben was getting close, a flurry late in the day seemed to have ended his chances. By the time they'd reached the car, the snow had stopped and Ben wondered if anyone would be prepared to go back. Like all good photographers, Mike and Ray were more than happy if it meant recording something exceptional. Back at the boulder, conditions were now perfect and Ben had it second try. It's called *Black Lung* after the colouration and shape of the rock, and in the US bouldering V-grade system is still rated V13 – equivalent to Font 8B. 'It's made my year,' Ben told Mike in the film he made of the trip.

Ben had been fully committed to the idea of settling with Jo in the US, at least for a while, so to watch S7 implode, albeit through no fault of his own, and consequently find himself back in Britain was a blow. 'I'm not sure what I was living on at that point,' Ben says. 'I had a good contract with Red Chilli and some savings.' He'd spent years living on next to nothing and still had a roof over his head, so in 2002 he simply started again, this time using his own name to create a new bouldering brand. More than ten years later it's still going strong.

Moon offers pretty much the same range of goods that Ben started selling with S7, but this time he has been wiser and trusted his own judgements more. Flying round the world to meet manufacturers and attend trade fairs has become part of his life, but the brand is much richer than its products. The kind of training advice that just didn't exist when Ben started climbing is now a regular feature of Moon's website. Over the years he's sponsored some of the best boulderers in the world, including Tyler Landman, the bouldering phenomenon who appeared, much as Ben had, as a teenager and quickly raced through the grades, making light work of Jerry Moffatt's Stanage classic *The Ace*, before going on to climb Font 8B+ and 8C. Ben acted as a mentor for Tyler, who has stepped back from his climbing while studying medicine in the States: 'Bouldering development really benefits from this kind of inspiration,' says Dan Varian. 'It all really helps bouldering stay alive as a sport.'

A year after he started his new company, Ben and Jo got married at the registry office on the King's Road in Chelsea, on the anniversary of his father's death – 30 November. It was a small wedding, with just thirty guests at the ceremony, half of them family. Jerry Moffatt was his best man. Jo was by then training as an acupuncturist, which she now practises in Sheffield. 'She's very patient,' Ben says. 'Very kind. I'm sure I'm not the easiest person to live with.' Their daughter Sylvie was born in 2009: 'She's incredibly determined physically,' Ben says. 'She's a bit of a tomboy and pretty fearless.' Both Jo and Ben have been absorbed seamlessly into each other's families, and Ben is close to his father-in-law. 'It's pretty good having him around; he worked in the steel industry as an engineer and is one of those guys who can fix everything.'

From the outside, it might have seemed that Ben was doing pretty much what he'd always done, living in Sheffield and going climbing. But in fact he'd pulled off a difficult transformation, restructuring his life to give him the space to have a proper relationship and run a business, while still doing what he loved best to an unbelievably high standard.

Now happily married and with Moon up and running, Ben looked for a problem to work on that he could fit in with his new family and new business. One line in particular stood out, at Burbage, ten minutes from his house in Sheffield. He'd been looking at this challenge for as long as he'd been going there, a miniature landmark just below the rim of the crag. The buttress had a bit of history; the 1970s gritstone god John Allen had climbed a route along the front of it. This only drew attention to the block's long and desperate lower lip. In some ways it was the perfect problem for Ben, not only close to home and fiendishly difficult, but physically suitable too. Gritstone is a superb bouldering medium, but at the upper end of the scale climbers are limited by the damage such coarse rock can do to their skin. 'I've got really good skin,' Ben says. 'It doesn't sweat much. It's quite dry but not so dry it splits easily. I'm lucky in that respect.' Even so, the abrasion meant he couldn't climb for long. 'The holds are sharp, and they're small. You can't try it for hours and hours. You'll cut your tips. You lose skin. I'd have to leave two or three days between each effort.'

Ben spent more than thirty days there in total – he can't recall exactly and his habit of keeping a record is long in the past – working first on the shorter version of the route, hanging the lip from a standing position. This he completed in 2005 and called *Voyager*. 'I went there with Zippy first in 2004 to have a play on it. I remember feeling the holds and thinking, this is doable. The standing start didn't take too long. I thought it was soft Font 8B.' The following year, in March 2006, he began his attempt to push the problem back into the base of *Voyager's* little buttress. This only added four moves to the problem, and the start is 'only' Font 8A. 'It doesn't sound like it should be that hard, but it does make a huge difference.' Those few who have repeated the stand-up version and then moved on to try the sit-down start have been surprised at how much these extra moves add to the overall process.

That's proved something of a relief to Ben. 'A lot of the time I was trying the sit-down start, I thought I was making heavy weather of it. I hadn't thought the stand-up was that hard. I'm glad I got it when I did. I was asking myself: "How long can you keep coming out here?"' Ben spent the winter months of 2005 and 2006 trying to complete the project and took it up again in the autumn, a few months after his fortieth birthday.

A few years before he'd separated his shoulder in a snowboarding accident in Utah, but despite the years and all those finger injuries, his body had proved amazingly resilient.

'You're so aware of your body throughout the whole process. Even just waking up in the morning. You go through your normal routine, the drive-out, doing the warm-up, always the same routine. There were a couple of arêtes and walls just behind the buttress, and I'd do those three or four times to get myself loose and moving. Go through that process enough times and you're really aware of how you feel. Whether the omens are good or bad. Struggling on the warm-up can put you in such a negative frame of mind. But if you feel good, then it's a struggle not getting too excited.'

Ben's friend 'Aussie' Gav Portman was at Burbage that day and caught the first ascent on video. There is better bouldering footage, but not much, given the context, that is quite as stirring. Here is the veteran fighter, enjoying one last moment of glory before he lets go for good. His reaction, even before he reaches the top of the boulder, is one of relief and profound joy. After *Hubble*, knowing success was close before he did it, he'd gone training, still uncertain of what he'd achieved. Watching him on top of *Voyager*, he knows precisely what it means, understands exactly the thin line between failure and success and roars with excitement.

'Did you think at forty you were running out of time?'

'That was part of it. You don't always know when you're going to do a problem. There are times when you feel good and it doesn't happen. Times when you get a hold right, but you've wasted a little bit of energy. Everything has to come together perfectly. I still felt good, but how long can you keep motivating yourself? I have a lot of motivation but it's not infinite. I spent a lot of time trying that low start over those three seasons. If you keep trying and don't succeed it can be pretty soul-destroying.'

Even now, over eight years later, the longer version of *Voyager* is still unrepeated and, at 8B+, it's still widely rated as the hardest boulder problem on Peak District gritstone and is one of the hardest problems in the UK.

'I didn't think it would go unrepeated for that long. It's a bit like *Hubble* in that respect. As time has passed I've felt more proud.'

'Did you ever figure out the rhyme and reason of feeling strong?'

'No. Sometimes you feel good, other times you don't. What you've done in the recent past has an impact; how many rest days, that kind of stuff. Sometimes you just feel light. Sometimes you feel you're moving well, and sometimes you don't. You're much better when you're doing things instinctively. It's a very Zen-type thing. That's why people use visualisation, to put you in that state of mind. You don't want to be talking to yourself when you're in the middle of something.'

It's impossible not to wonder what Jeremy Moon would have thought, watching this shaky sequence of his son on a rock climb of such incredible difficulty. Given his interest in choreography, given the abstract structure of holds and the process of running a human body across them, like code through a cipher, it's reasonable to think he'd be intrigued. It doesn't really matter whether climbing is more sport that art – or vice versa. It is what you want to make of it. *Hoop-La* hangs in the Tate; *Voyager* sits above the Burbage valley. Ben often draws an analogy between climbing and activities where you perform a routine: dance, which his father had studied, and especially gymnastics: 'Except that judges prescribe moves in gymnastics. Boulder problems are created by nature. By the time you're linking moves together it's a bit like a gymnastics routine and if you get ten out of ten then you'll do the problem. Get nine and you fall. But the rock is your judge.'

Voyager. **Photo:** Adam Long.

Ben on the Cuillin Ridge, Isle of Skye. **Photo**: Ben Pritchard.

EPILOGUE

It's the first weekend in October 2013, and Raven Tor is buzzing. At its right-hand end, where much of the best bouldering is found, there's a continuous line of bouldering mats, like a bed for a very long snake, and a crowd of toned young things, some girls but mostly boys, debating sequences, urging each other on. Further along the crag, the atmosphere is more serious. Here climbers are working their projects, practising moves, making links, building towards the point where a redpoint is a realistic prospect. Ryan Pasquill is pasted on the blank white wall of *Mutation*, currently the hardest sport climb in the Peak District and also one of the best. His fingers are clamped to the route's famous crux sequence, a wrong-handed crossover, which he makes but then is defeated by a long stretch above. Lowering off, he flicks his long fringe out of his eyes and smiles shyly, mentioning something about such a tough move coming on top of the previous sequence. Now thirty years old, Ryan is one of the best rock climbers of his generation. He's made bold and dangerous on-sights and first ascents on gritstone, and earlier in 2013 climbed his first 9a, at Siurana.

Untying his rope, Ryan pulls it through the line of quickdraws and takes his turn belaying for Mina Leslie-Wujastyk, who sets off up *Evolution*, the truncated and, at 8c+ to *Mutation's* 9a, slightly easier version of the same route. Her style is fluid and dynamic, her legs and hips working faster and more flexibly than her male counterparts to make more of whatever footholds are available on the blank and overhanging wall. Where *Evolution* leads slightly left, and *Mutation* continues straight up, she slaps for a good finger pocket and just misses, spinning off into space. Mina is recently returned from a bouldering festival in Västervik, Sweden, flying there after competing at an event in Stuttgart. Two days before that, she'd arrived home from a six-week climbing trip to South Africa, where she was bouldering Font 8A+. Given she competes for Britain on the World Cup circuit, this off-season life is actually quite laid-back to the usual round of airports and hotels. She shares this modern rock-star life on her popular blog; if you want to watch some of her hardest climbs, they are there on Vimeo and YouTube; if you want to follow her latest progress she's there on Facebook and Twitter too.

It's fair to say that sport climbing is back in fashion.

Standing under Martin Atkinson's 1980s classic *Mecca*, rubbing his fingers, Ben seems more than at home in this latest version of the vertical life; the climbing world has changed dramatically in his long career, but it's a revolution he helped instigate, and so why wouldn't he feel comfortable here? He nods towards a climber at the other end of the crag using a clip-stick to reach a bolt high above his head so he can practise the next moves on a top-rope. 'Quite practical, really,' he says, strapping a kneepad around his leg. Just as gear evolves, so do climbing techniques, and the fierce groove of *Mecca* now yields to an elegant knee-bar – hence the pad.

It used to be that climbers got older and, while their achievements were honoured, after two or three decades their life's best had become classics accessible to the masses. That hasn't happened with the harder sport routes from the 1980s and 1990s. They're still hard. *Evolution* was the last great contribution Jerry Moffatt made to sport climbing, in 1995. Steve McClure climbed *Mutation* in 1998. Just to the left, Ben's own route, *Hubble*, will go into the new climbing guidebook at 9a. After twenty-three years it's still had only a handful of ascents. These routes came from a time when British rock climbers were the best in the world, something you would struggle to argue now. So there's a lot of respect from the younger climbers, even, from some, an edgy excitement when they register who it is they're watching. Ben must seem a little austere to the youngsters, quite old school. These days, the fashionable phrase is borrowed from Spanish climbers: 'A muerte!' – to the death. Passionate abandon is not really how Ben ever did things, but who knows, maybe, like the clip-stick, it's something he'll adopt.

Rubbing the soles of his boots, he steps on to the rock and pulls on to a flat, wide spike at the start of *Mecca*. He did Martin's route earlier in the summer as a warm-up for the longer, extended version, another of Steve McClure's creations, which pushed the grade up to 8c, but he moans about his memory as he hesitates over a move that should be familiar. It's the only fluff he makes. He has to work hard in the groove, but otherwise Ben is precise and smooth. The alpinist and sport climber Andy Cave is holding his rope. The two of them often climb together, and with daughters the same age also find themselves sneaking off from shared family holidays to do a route. 'He has this astonishing base level of around 7c,' Andy says. 'You watch him and everything he does is so precise. Nothing is wasted. Every move is as good as it can be.' Ben tells him to stop gossiping. He's reached the top of *Mecca*, and is shaking out before continuing on to Steve's *Extension*.

Although it's quite cold, and the friction is consequently pretty good for Raven Tor, Ben is now overheating and pulls off his t-shirt. He's obviously in good shape, but his skin is a little creased and lacks the smooth vibrancy of the younger climbers around him. It's moving and also impressive to see a forty-seven-year-old man climbing this hard. Then he's off again, exact and elegant. Near the top of the wall, working his way into a slender groove, he bounces his right hand up and then slots his right heel onto a hold almost at waist height, but the shape isn't quite right and he falls. He's not far off, but he expected to have done this route by now; moving house and business commitments have kept him busy this summer.

Inevitably, when he talks about who inspires him in the modern era the names of Adam Ondra and Chris Sharma crop up, especially Ondra, who has driven the sport forward most in the very recent past. 'Adam seems in a different league.' The idea that Alex Megos can climb 9a on sight, or take only two days to repeat the Australian Font 8C+ boulder problem *Wheel of Life*, is genuinely exciting: 'I watch Sylvie and other young kids at the wall, and I realise we've only just started. How could you not be a good climber? I didn't begin climbing properly until I was fifteen or sixteen. Adam was climbing from a very young age; it's a massive boost. Things are going to get ridiculous. It's really a question of how much a human tendon can take.'

Looking back, he spins through the names of those who impressed or influenced him. Many of them are still famous: Jerry Moffatt, Marc and Antoine Le Menestrel, Patrick Edlinger and Wolfgang Güllich, the latter pair prematurely lost to us. 'Malcolm Smith and Stuart Cameron were the strongest climbers I ever met. Stuart was probably stronger than Malc, but didn't have the application or focus. He did some great stuff but could have done more. Malc maybe got sucked into the training.' Staying on course as a climber has never been easy, but sport climbing at the highest level, as Ben knows only too well, is a fine line between preparation that borders on the pathological and rare moments of perfection.

Ben hasn't given up on the mountains either. In the summer he was in the Dolomites, climbing with David Falt, who looks after Moon's social media from his base in Briançon. They were trying a route called *Akut*, 500 metres long on the Cima Ovest di Lavaredo with a pitch of 8a. Ben and David fixed the first three rope-lengths and then tried to climb the remaining twelve in a day but were stopped by the crux tenth pitch, a wildly exposed overhang. 'Oh God, I was so tired by the end,' he says, bringing to mind the image of a racehorse pulling a plough all day.

After finishing the low start to *Voyager*, Ben had thought he was more or less done with climbing, at least at an elite level. With a business to run and a young child, long periods of travel were no longer possible and there didn't seem to be a project in the Peak District that inspired him in the same way. Andy says Ben would turn up at the wall for a Christmas get-together, having not climbed for months, and still burn everyone off. He followed Jerry's example and did some surfing, but his attachment to climbing finally proved too strong and he made the decision to take it more seriously again. It's quite hard to turn your back on something that made sense to you as a seven-year-old. It's not that Ben necessarily has regrets; it's more he senses some potential deep inside that he hasn't yet exploited.

'What do you want to climb? If you could have one or two routes what would they be?'

He nods up at *Mutation*. 'It's such a beautiful piece of rock,' he says, and the fierce crux would suit him. 'Or *Rainshadow* at Malham. That looks a brilliant route.' He adds quietly: 'Steve was the man.'

He says: 'I want to climb 9a, although I'm starting to doubt a little whether I can. My lifestyle isn't quite sorted out yet. Nic [Sellars] said I would. Apparently Steve [Lewis] told Zippy I should be climbing 9c, I'm that strong.' He laughs at this.

'It seems likely, you did 9a already.'

'Yeah, maybe,' he admits, but doesn't sound totally at ease with that idea. There's always something more – as W. H. Murray might have said – to contain.

SIGNIFICANT DATES
AND ASCENTS

This list is a collection of selected highlights from Ben's climbing career, together with other key dates in his life.

FA = First Ascent

1966, 13 Jun	Born Benedick Joseph Moon.
1973, 30 Nov	**Father** Jeremy killed in a motorcycle accident.
1974	Goes climbing for the first time while on a family holiday in the Lake District.
1982	Christ's Hospital school trip to the Alps, with Ric Potter.
1982	Leaves school, aged sixteen.
1984, Apr	Strawberries (E7 6b, FA: Ron Fawcett, 1980), Tremadog, Wales.
1984, Jun	**FA**: Statement of Youth (F8a), Lower Pen Trwyn, Wales. *Aged only eighteen, Ben made the first ascent of what was then one of the most difficult routes in England.*
1985	Revelations (F8a+, FA: Jerry Moffatt, 1984), Raven Tor, England.
1985	Chouca (F8a+, FA: Antoine Le Menestrel, 1984), Buoux, France. *Third ascent.*
1986	**FA**: Zeke the Freak (F8b), Rubicon Wall, England.
1986	La Rose et le Vampire (F8b, FA: Antoine Le Menestrel, 1985), Buoux, France.
1987	**FA**: Pump Up The Power (F8a+), Raven Tor, England.
1987	**FA**: The Thing (Font 8A), Cressbrook, England.
1988, Apr	Le Spectre du Sur-mutant (F8b+, FA: Jean-Baptiste Tribout, 1988), Buoux, France.
1988, Apr	Le Minimum (F8b+, FA: Marc Le Menestrel, 1986), Buoux, France.
1988, Apr	La Rage de Vivre (F8b+, FA: Antoine Le Menestrel, 1986.) Buoux, France. *In the space of nine days, Ben climbs the three hardest routes in France.*
1989, Jan	**FA**: Agincourt (F8c), Buoux, France. *The first F8c in France. 'When 6c just isn't that hard any more and 6b is approaching a rest.'*
1989, Nov	**FA**: Maginot Line (F8c), Volx, France.

SIGNIFICANT ASCENTS AND DATES

1990, 14 Jun	**FA**: Hubble (F9a), Raven Tor, England. *Originally graded F8c+ (the world's first), it is now increasingly regarded as the world's first F9a route. Jerry Moffatt's route Liquid Ambar at Lower Pen Trwyn, originally F8c and now F8c+, is now likely the world's first F8c+ route.*
1991	**On-sight**: Kleinian Envy, Dinorwig Quarry, Wales.
1991	Liquid Ambar (F8c+, FA: Jerry Moffatt, 1990), Lower Pen Trwyn, Wales. *Second ascent of Jerry Moffatt's route. It would wait a further eighteen years for a third ascent, from Pete Robins.*
1993	**FA**: Sea of Tranquility (F8c+), Lower Pen Trwyn, Wales. *Originally graded F8c.*
1993	Dominator (Font 8A+, FA: Jerry Moffatt, 1993), Yosemite, USA. *Second ascent of Jerry Moffatt's Camp 4 boulder problem. Also climbs Midnight Lightning and Stick It, and flashes The Force, Thriller and After Midnight on the same trip.*
1994	**FA**: Superman Sit-start (Font 8B/+), Cressbrook, England.
1994	**FA**: Pinch II (Font 8B), Stoney Middleton, England. *Immortalised in the film One Summer.*
1994	**FA**: Ben's Extension (Font 8A), Stanage, England.
1995	**On-sight**: En Un Combat Douteux (F8a), Cimai, France.
1995	Macumba Club (F8c, FA: Jean-Baptiste Tribout, 1992), Orgon, France.
1995	Bronx (F8c+, FA: François Petit, 1994), Orgon, France. *Second ascent.*
1995	Superplafond (F8c+, FA: Jean-Baptiste Tribout, 1994), Volx, France. *Second ascent.*
1996	Karma (Font 8A/+, FA: Fred Nicole, 1995), Fontainebleau, France.
2000	**FA**: Black Lung (Font 8B), Joe's Valley, USA.
2000	**FA**: 8 Ball (Font 8B), Gardom's Edge, England.
2002, 30 Nov	**Marries** Joanne Arthur on the King's Road, Chelsea.
2004	**FA**: Cypher (Font 8B), Slipstones, England.
2005	The Ace (Font 8B, FA: Jerry Moffatt, 2002), Stanage, England. *Second ascent of Jerry Moffatt's problem.*
2005	High Fidelity (Font 8B, FA: Steve Dunning, 2005), Caley, England. *Second ascent shortly after the first ascent.*
2005	**FA**: Voyager (Font 8B), Burbage, England.
2006	**Flash**: Diaphanous Sea (Font 8A+, FA: Fred Nicole, 1990s), Hueco Tanks, USA.
2006	**FA**: Voyager Sit-start (Font 8B+), Burbage, England. *Unrepeated at the time of publication.*
2007	Cuillin Ridge, Isle of Skye, Scotland. *With Ben Pritchard, Ben Tetler, Rob Moon and Chris Plant.*
2009, 12 Jan	**Daughter** Sylvie born.
2013	Mecca Extension (F8c, FA: Steve McClure, 1998), Raven Tor, England.

ACKNOWLEDGEMENTS

When people heard I was writing about Ben Moon, they often told me that he is a nice guy; this is undoubtedly true, but he is also determined, even steely, when faced with a goal. He thinks clearly about climbing, cuts away the excess and (almost always) remains calm. As a role model to any young climber, he is exemplary. Even when, at the height of his powers, he failed on a route, and exploded in frustration, there was something controlled about it, like a neutron bomb, expending energy but causing no physical damage.

The only negative thing I can say is that he's a Chelsea fan. Nobody's perfect. The commitment and mental focus required to be a top climber certainly hasn't got any less over the years, but Ben's generation was the first to be so dedicated and without the widespread acceptance in the broader climbing community that this is how things need to be. He saw the future, and set about realising it, over two decades. Getting to know someone like that, and gaining an insight into the life of a true athlete was

ACKNOWLEDGEMENTS

a great privilege. I owe an immense debt to Ben himself for his patience
and openness throughout the project. When I felt telling his story – and
this is very much his story – required a different approach to the one we'd
begun, he pondered the issue and agreed and we were able to continue.
I'm also indebted to his family, his wife Jo, his brother Rob and his sister
Georgina, his mother Beth and his uncle David. When I needed to fill
gaps in Ben's memory a number of his friends helped me out, particularly
his school-friend Ric Potter, bouldering partner Ben Pritchard and the
photographer Ray Wood. John Varney helped me with a few details from
the aftermath of Jeremy's accident, and Zoe Brown, who recalled days in
Cowlishaw Road. I'm grateful to some climbers who came after, notably
Steve McClure and Dan Varian. I'd also like to thank: Andy Cave, Neil
Foster, Alun Hughes, Gill Kent, Marc Le Menestrel and Tony Ryan,
for delving into the past. And Jon Barton and John Coefield, essentially
for being there.

INDEX

INDEX